Effective Business Writing In A Week

Martin Manser

The Teach Yourself series has been trusted around the world
for over 60 years. This series of 'In A Week' business books is
designed to help people at all levels and around the world to
further th̶   rts learn in
a lifetime

I wish to thank Linda Eley for her careful typing of my manuscript, Benny Manser, Su Hlyan Htet, Michael Allmey and Sarah Peasley for their helpful contributions and Bernard Harlock for his constructive comments.

Martin Manser is an expert writer with a unique combination of skills and experience. He has compiled or edited over 200 reference books on the English language, Bible reference and business skills in a 30-year professional career. He is an English-language specialist and teaches English to business colleagues: participants in his courses find them to be a safe place to ask questions and for participants' confidence to grow. Since 2002 he has also been a language consultant and trainer, leading courses in business communications for national and international companies and organizations on report writing, project management and time management.

Website: www.martinmanser.co.uk

Effective
Business Writing

Martin Manser

www.inaweek.co.uk

First published in Great Britain in 2013 by Hodder & Stoughton. An Hachette UK company.

This edition published 2013

Copyright © Martin Manser 2013

The right of Martin Manser to be identified as the Author of the Work has been asserted by him in accordance with the Copyright, Designs and Patents Act 1988.

Database right Hodder & Stoughton (makers)

The *Teach Yourself* name is a registered trademark of Hachette UK.

British Library Cataloguing in Publication Data: a catalogue record for this title is available from the British Library.

10 9 8 7 6 5 4 3 2 1

The publisher has used its best endeavours to ensure that any website addresses referred to in this book are correct and active at the time of going to press. However, the publisher and the author have no responsibility for the websites and can make no guarantee that a site will remain live or that the content will remain relevant, decent or appropriate.

The publisher has made every effort to mark as such all words which it believes to be trademarks. The publisher should also like to make it clear that the presence of a word in the book, whether marked or unmarked, in no way affects its legal status as a trademark.

Every reasonable effort has been made by the publisher to trace the copyright holders of material in this book. Any errors or omissions should be notified in writing to the publisher, who will endeavour to rectify the situation for any reprints and future editions.

Typeset by Cenveo® Publisher Services.

Printed and bound in Great Britain by CPI Group (UK) Ltd., Croydon, CR0 4YY.

Hodder & Stoughton policy is to use papers that are natural, renewable and recyclable products and made from wood grown in sustainable forests. The logging and manufacturing processes are expected to conform to the environmental regulations of the country of origin.

Hodder & Stoughton Ltd

338 Euston Road

London NW1 3BH

www.hodder.co.uk

Also available in ebook

Contents

Introduction

Most of us spend hours every day typing emails and other documents at work, yet how many of us have ever had any training in writing skills? The result is that we write emails and reports that aren't clear. Precious time is then wasted as colleagues need to ask us to clarify what we meant.

Even though we may use many different ways of communicating (e.g. texting, tweeting, Facebook®, LinkedIn®) many of us would benefit from help in writing clearer business emails and reports. Or perhaps you have been asked to lead a presentation in a few days' time and you don't know where to begin. Or you may find yourself having to write advertising copy or press releases, and you want to know the basics. Finally, many companies and organizations want to engage successfully online by building and maintaining a website and using social media (blogs, Twitter®, Facebook, LinkedIn, etc.) effectively, but where do you begin and what are the key points to know?

All these situations call for effective writing skills and it is my hope that you will find this book to be a reliable guide. And if you think you have already mastered the foundation level, then I hope to provide you with further techniques to encourage you to become an even more accomplished writer.

In this week we will cover:

Sunday: Plan your writing well. Don't launch straight into writing, but think and plan carefully first.

Monday: Edit your text thoroughly. Resist the temptation to press 'send'; read through your text carefully, checking and revising it.

Tuesday: Write effective emails and reports. Make sure that both the content and tone of your documents are appropriate.

Wednesday: Give excellent presentations by preparing both your message and yourself thoroughly.

Thursday: Write persuasively in a fresh way, when drafting text for advertisements and press releases.

Friday: Build a successful website that is targeted at your intended readers/users and will fulfil the purposes you have outlined.

Saturday: Use social media effectively to build and develop business contacts, exchange information and discuss ideas.

Each day of the week covers a different area and begins with an introduction to what the day is about. The main material that follows explains the key lessons by clarifying important principles, which are backed up by tips, case studies, etc. Each day concludes with a summary, follow-up exercise and multiple-choice questions, to reinforce the learning points.

The principles I outline here are the fruit of over 30 years in business, particularly in the area of writing, and over ten years in leading courses on business communications. As I have reflected on participants' responses to the workshops I have led, two comments have recurred: 'You gave me more confidence' and 'The workshop was a refresher course'. My hope therefore is that as you read and act on what I write, it will not only be a refresher course but will also give you fresh confidence to be a more effective communicator at work.

Martin Manser
August 2013

SUNDAY

Plan your writing well

There's more to writing than just typing out words on your keyboard and then pressing 'send'. What we're looking at today is planning and preparing what you want to write before you type anything on your computer.

It's rather like decorating a room – you can't wait to start putting on a new coat of paint, but you know that it won't last long unless you prepare all the surfaces in advance. So today is about planning your writing carefully.

We're going to look at:

the basic aims in communicating: if you know where you are going, you are more likely to arrive at your destination than if you wander aimlessly

the writing process. Notice the word 'process'; there are several different steps in writing: thinking and organizing your material; writing your first draft; and checking and editing your first draft.

Today (and Monday) are all about writing in general before we come to the details of writing specific kinds of document. If you master these basic steps, then you will have laid a secure foundation and you will be in a strong position to tackle any writing task. From Tuesday onwards, we will look at different kinds of writing.

The basics of communication

I often begin my workshops on business writing with the memory prompt 'AIR':

- **A**udience
- **I**ntention
- **R**esponse

> **TIP** *There is more to business writing than just typing an email and then pressing 'send'.*

Audience

'Audience' means know who you want to communicate with. The key point is that the focus is not on you, but on the person/people you are trying to communicate with. This means the question you should ask yourself is not so much, 'What should I say/write?', but 'What do my audience need to hear?' To answer that question well, you need to think about who your audience is and what their response to your communication is likely to be.

What do you know about your audience?

- age and gender
- educational level and language (e.g. native English speaker or not?)
- position in an organization
- background/likes/dislikes (here you could be specific, e.g. a favourite website, television programme, radio station, magazine)
- strengths and weaknesses
- knowledge of, and interest in, what you are communicating
- likely response to your message.

Of course, not all of these will be relevant to every communication you make, but the more significant ones should be at the back of your mind to enable you to communicate successfully.

Who you are writing to should affect the way in which you write. For example, are you writing to your boss? Or someone who has written in to your company or organization with a complaint? In each case, how you express what you are trying to say will be different.

If you are emailing your boss, you may simply give him or her the information that he or she has asked for:

Hi Sally

Sales for 2012 were 10 per cent up on 'Introduction to Project Management'. We have sold just over 3000 copies and we reprinted a further 1000 copies of that title last month.

Harry

Your boss wants the information quickly, with no extras. If you are responding to a complaint, however, your tone will be different:

Dear Mrs Brown,

Thank you for taking the trouble to write to us to express your disappointment with the service you recently received at one of our restaurants. I am very sorry that you found our service unsatisfactory.

I have checked the details from your letter and it appears that the member of staff you dealt with on 3 October at our Grantchester restaurant was a temporary worker. He was unfamiliar with our company policy on the high levels of service we require from all our staff.

I have now taken the necessary steps to ensure that such a situation will not occur again.

Thank you again for writing. Please be assured that we aim to offer our customers the highest possible level of service at all times.

Yours sincerely,

John Duckworth

Do you see the difference? The email to your boss is short and to the point. The letter responding to the complaint is expanded and also crucially the *tone* is much softer.

So you need to know who your audience is. When I am preparing a talk, I often think of one or two people I know who will be in the audience – and I gauge how they are likely to receive what I am saying, their present level of understanding and the point I want them to reach by the end of my talk.

The importance of listening
How can you learn more about your audience? By *listening*. Listening:

- focuses on the other person. Often when someone else is talking, we're focusing on thinking about what we are going to say as a reply.
- values the person you are listening to as an individual in their own right, so that you understand 'where they're coming from', why they are working or speaking as they are.
- helps you understand the point at which a person is. For example, if you are trying to sell something to customers, you want to build a good relationship with them. By listening, you will discern who is interested and who is not, so you can use your time more valuably and concentrate on the likelier potential clients.
- encourages you to ask the right questions. As you focus on the other person (not yourself), you will want to know more. We can distinguish:

- closed questions: ones that can be answered by a straight 'Yes' or 'No': 'Was the project late?' 'Yes.' 'Will you be able to give me the figures by 5.00 pm?' 'No.'
- open questions: ones that get people talking. Open questions begin with *why*, *how*, *who*, *when*, *where*, *what*. 'Why do you think the project is running late?' 'Because we didn't plan in enough time for the extra work the customer now wants.' Most of the questions you should ask as a manager should be open questions.

● means that you listen not only to the words a colleague is saying but also perceive their response to what you are saying by being sensitive to their body language and tone of voice.

● allows you to 'listen between the lines', to become aware of any underlying messages – your response could be, for instance, 'So I guess what you're saying is that you need someone else to help you complete this task on time.'

● allows you to distinguish between facts and opinions. You will hear both, and you can discern what is objective information and what are the subjective thoughts about such information. You are then in a position to evaluate what has been said.

● enables you to gather information so that you can solve problems and make decisions more efficiently.

● builds trust between people: you show that you are genuinely interested in them. This forms the basis that helps you to work well with them. Listening often improves relationships. Rather than someone keeping angry feelings to himself/herself and becoming increasingly tense, listening – and allowing someone to speak openly about their difficulties – provides a release for them.

Selling benefits not features

Nigel was a wise salesman. He knew his products thoroughly but he resisted the temptation simply to tell his customers the new technical features of his products (e.g. their updated design and faster processing). Instead, he put himself in his customers' place, and constantly asked himself how they would benefit from the new products, i.e. what they would gain from each of the new features,

> such as greater efficiency from the new design, saving time because of faster processing. In this way, he not only gained their interest but also won sales.

Intention

By 'Intention' I mean the message: the key point(s) you want to put over. In the examples mentioned earlier, the key points in an email to your boss were stated very briefly, and the intention in replying to the letter of complaint was to defuse the writer's anger and say that you had looked into the matter.

If you are selling a product or service, you need to be clear on what its unique selling proposition (USP) is, the particular feature that distinguishes it from your competitors.

You may face some difficulties in identifying what the intention/message of your communication is.

- You may not know it yourself. If this is the case, *think*. To take an example, my website was recently down and I was without one, so it made me think: What is the purpose of my website? Do I want people simply to find out about me and my services, or buy books from me, or contact me with questions? Think hard until you can identify your key messages definitely and precisely. We will explore this crucial area of thinking and the role of spider diagrams or mind maps later today.
- Is your message clear? If it isn't clear to you, then it will hardly be clear to those you are trying to communicate with. On one of my writing courses I discovered that the key message of one document was buried in a 67-word sentence in brackets near the end of the document!
- Even if you do know what your key message is, you may need to explain some background to that key message before you can get to it.

Response

What do you want the person you are communicating with to do with your communication? Sometimes we can be so preoccupied with working out all the details of what we are trying to say that we forget what we want our readers to do with the information we give them. You may simply be providing the people you are writing to with information, but it is more likely that you want them to make some kind of a decision.

Is it crystal clear how they are to respond? What are the next steps you want them to take? For example, if you are writing a fund-raising email, you need to include in clear terms:

- how your readers can donate money, e.g. on which website
- what bank account codes to use, if relevant
- how donors can gift-aid their contributions.

The writing process

It is important to note that there are steps to be taken in writing; it isn't simply a matter of typing an email with the first thing that comes into your mind and then pressing 'send'!

We can break down the writing process into different steps:

- thinking and planning
- writing your first draft
- editing your draft.

Each of these will take about a third of the time you have allocated to writing a document. Note especially that editing your draft may take you significantly longer than you thought.

We will look at the first two of these today and the third in the Monday chapter.

Thinking

Bearing in mind the results of your AIR (Audience, Intention, Response) analysis, think about what you want to write. One good way of helping you to start thinking about what to write is to draw a spider diagram (also known as a mind map). Take a blank piece of A4 paper. Arrange it in landscape position (i.e. lengthwise) and write the subject matter of the report in the middle. (Write a word or few words, but not a whole sentence.) You may find it helpful to work in pencil, as you can rub out what you write if necessary.

Now write around your central word(s) the different key aspects that come to your mind, maybe as a result of your reading. It is important not to list the ideas in order of importance; simply write them down. To begin with, you do not need to join the ideas up with lines linking connected items.

If you get stuck at any point, ask yourself the question words *why*, *how*, *what*, *who*, *when*, *where* and *how much*. These will set you

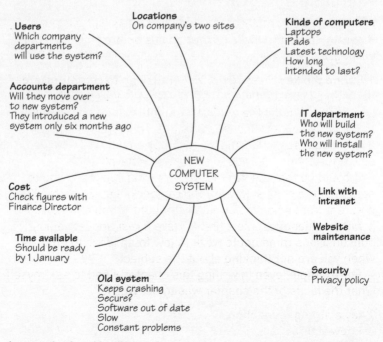

Users
Which company
departments
will use the system?

Locations
On company's two sites

Kinds of computers
Laptops
iPads
Latest technology
How long
intended to last?

Accounts department
Will they move over
to new system?
They introduced a new
system only six months ago

IT department
Who will build
the new system?
Who will install
the new system?

NEW COMPUTER SYSTEM

Cost
Check figures with
Finance Director

**Link with
intranet**

**Website
maintenance**

Time available
Should be ready
by 1 January

Old system
Keeps crashing
Secure?
Software out of date
Slow
Constant problems

Security
Privacy policy

An example of a spider diagram for a report on buying new computer systems

thinking. The important point to notice about the thinking stage is that if you undertake this step, then when you come to writing later on, you won't be daunted by a blank screen or a blank piece of paper as you will already know what it is you are writing about.

When I do this, I am often amazed at:

● how easy the task is: it doesn't feel like work! The ideas and concepts seem to flow naturally and spontaneously.
● how valuable that piece of paper is. I have captured all (or at least some or many) of the key points. I don't want to lose that piece of paper!

Probably, the most fruitful question word to answer is 'why'. Why am I writing this? I find it a good discipline to ask myself this often when I write as it makes me examine the context of my document.

Planning and drafting

After you have completed the thinking stages with a spider diagram, there are three further stages before you can begin writing.

1 Refine the key message(s) you are trying to communicate

In writing, I constantly ask myself, 'What am I really trying to say?' or 'What is the one key thought I want my audience to know?' If you are unsure about this, try to discuss it with a colleague face to face (rather than by email) so that your colleague challenges you to think more sharply.

It could be that the key message of what you are trying to say is not the central idea on your spider diagram; it could be different from what you originally thought. If you can't discuss it with a colleague, take a break. Have a rest and let your subconscious mind get to work. Allow fresh ideas to emerge when you are not thinking about the subject.

For example, even in writing this chapter, I had to ask myself what the focus of the chapter was to be. Was it:

1 lay a strong foundation
2 know your aims
3 plan your writing well.

SUNDAY

MONDAY

TUESDAY

WEDNESDAY

THURSDAY

FRIDAY

SATURDAY

Clearly, each of these is an important aspect, but I settled (after a good night's sleep!) on '3 plan your writing well' with '2 know your aims' being an important expression of that and '1 lay a strong foundation' as the result of that.

Refining your message can take some time and if you find it difficult, at least eliminate parts that are less important. For example, if you are analysing the disadvantages of a former computer system, then the exact technical details of the old software are probably less significant than the fact that it has serious drawbacks, is out of date and no longer fulfils its original purpose.

To work out what your key message is, you also need to consider your document's audience and response. If you are writing a report for your Finance Director, for example, you will want to present the financial facts (e.g. cost, return on investment) as your key message. However, if your Finance Director has already given the go-ahead to installing the new system and you are writing a report for colleagues in Research and Development who will be using the system, then your approach will be different. Your key message may then be the usability of the new system and its advantages compared to the old one.

2 Develop your phrases

Before you organize your thoughts, here is an additional stage. The key words in your spider diagram are probably nouns (names of things). The aim is to add a verb (doing word) to make a more powerful combination. For example a draft on an article about giving presentations might include the following:

You could add verbs to give:

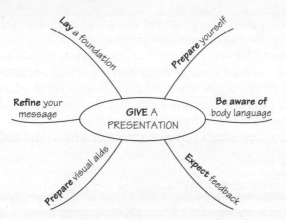

And even go to a third stage and begin to add adjectives (describing words) to give:

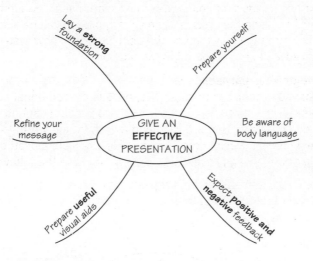

Do you see? What we are trying to do is spread the load of the core meaning: rather than simply 'visual aids' we end up with 'prepare useful visual aids'.

Use a thesaurus and/or a dictionary of collocations (word partners) to develop your words and phrases. Work on them, hone them, sculpture them so they clearly express what you want (*expect positive and negative* feedback; *refine* your message).

The key point here is that you are preparing well: you are preparing the most important phrases in your document so that when it comes to the writing stage, you will face a blank screen or a blank piece of paper with strong phrases already in place that will form the central parts of your message. These phrases could also form the basis for headings in the final document:

● Laying a strong foundation
● Refining your message.

3 Organize your information

Arrange the information you are giving in a certain order. The aim here is to find the most appropriate, logical way to present what you want to say. Ways include:

● arranging in terms of importance, probably listing the most important first
● comparing the advantages and disadvantages
● analysing different aspects of a scheme, e.g. political, legal, social, economic, financial
● taking in a chronological approach – considering a time sequence.

So you could number the points on your spider diagram in the order in which you could deal with them. You may change your mind as you write – that doesn't matter; the important thing is to settle in your mind approximately what order you will tackle the different aspects of the subject that you have listed.

We will deal further with arranging items in a logical order in the Tuesday chapter.

Summary

Today we have looked at preparing to write by planning well, looking at:

the general principles underlying all communication: the need to consider your audience, your intention (message) and the response you want from your audience

the importance of listening so that you can know more about the colleagues you want to communicate with

the writing process: the steps underlying every significant document you write, examining initially the process of thinking and organizing your thoughts.

SUNDAY

MONDAY

TUESDAY

WEDNESDAY

THURSDAY

FRIDAY

SATURDAY

Fact-check [answers at the back]

1. Thinking about the basics of communication, the letters AIR stand for:
   a) Abbreviations, Image, Reputation ❏
   b) Activity, Information, Reflection ❏
   c) Attachments, Internet, Receptivity ❏
   d) Audience, Intention, Response ❏

2. Knowing who you are communicating to is:
   a) a waste of time ❏
   b) vital ❏
   c) unnecessary ❏
   d) quite important ❏

3. What you are trying to communicate should be:
   a) vague ❏
   b) ambiguous ❏
   c) confusing ❏
   d) clear ❏

4. When writing an email, I try to work out in advance:
   a) the response I want my reader to make ❏
   b) nothing; I just type what comes into my head ❏
   c) what to have for lunch ❏
   d) the 15 possible responses my reader could make ❏

5. You've forgotten to think about what response you want from the email you're about to send. Should you:
   a) press 'send', knowing they can email back if they want to pursue it ❏
   b) hope that the recipient will not notice ❏
   c) rewrite the email before you press 'send' ❏
   d) tell your boss about it tomorrow ❏

6. When selling a new product or service, you should emphasize:
   a) its new features ❏
   b) its benefits to your customers ❏
   c) its disadvantages ❏
   d) its cost ❏

7. Listening:
   a) is a waste of time; I just want to express myself ❏
   b) is a useful tool so I know what people are thinking ❏
   c) is such hard work that I don't really bother ❏
   d) makes me angry so I don't bother ❏

8. Before beginning to write a report:
   a) I just launch straight into writing ❏
   b) I get so bogged down in the details that I forget my key thoughts ❏
   c) I spend time planning my key messages ❏
   d) I don't bother to plan at all ❏

9. I spend time organizing my key thoughts in a business document:
   a) constantly ❑
   b) rarely ❑
   c) never ❑
   d) when I feel like it ❑

10. To stop and think about what exactly you are trying to communicate is:
    a) a luxury ❑
    b) essential ❑
    c) a nice-to-have ❑
    d) a waste of time ❑

Follow-up

1 Think of an effective document that you wrote. Why was it successful?

  A Who was the audience: who were you communicating with?

  I Intention: what was your message? What were you trying to say?

  R Response: what response did you receive?

Why was it successful? How do you know?

2 Think of a document that you have written that was not successful. Why was it not successful?

  A Who was the audience: who were you communicating with?

  I Intention: what was your message? What were you trying to say?

  R Response: what response did you receive?

Why was it not successful? How do you know?

SUNDAY

MONDAY

TUESDAY

WEDNESDAY

THURSDAY

FRIDAY

SATURDAY

MONDAY

Edit
your text
thoroughly

You should allow some time to elapse between writing your first draft and then checking it, whenever possible. The intervening time can be as short as a break for coffee or as long as a few days, but when you come to check your text, your thinking might be: 'Who wrote this – it isn't bad' or, more likely, 'Who wrote this – it's awful'.

For example, on checking your document, you may find that you have written too much about something that on further reflection was not very important. Or you may realize that you have not written enough about something more important. Now is the time to redress that balance. Don't leave it as it is, hoping for the best and leaving the readers to sort out what you are trying to say. Remember that if your text isn't clear to you (when you have spent some time on writing it), it won't be clear to your readers.

Today we discuss the need to read through your text again, checking it, revising it and changing certain words and phrases.

Let's look at certain techniques you can use to check the documents you write.

Make sure your text is accurate

Recently, I was checking a costing I had written for a publisher and discovered to my horror that for some reason I had written down numbers that were half what they should be. Fortunately, I managed to correct the error before I sent it off. And we've all received emails inviting us to a meeting on Tuesday 14 September, only to discover that 14 September is a Wednesday. The result is that many colleagues spend precious time emailing requests for clarification and then having to respond to them with the exact date. It would have been better if the person who originally sent the message had checked the details before sending it.

So: read through your text. Are all facts, e.g. dates, sums of money, spellings of names, correct? George Stephenson (railway engineer); Robert Louis Stevenson (Scottish writer). Do percentages in a table or chart add up to 100 per cent (i.e. not 91 per cent or 110 per cent): you will lose credibility if you are wrong.

Don't simply check what is there. Also check what isn't there too. Have you missed out vital logical steps in your argument?

TIP *If your text isn't clear to you, it won't be clear to your readers.*

Make sure your text is grammatical

'A box of pencils *are* on the table' or '*is* on the table?' Our brain may say the plural 'pencils' should be followed by the plural *are*, but grammatically, the correct form is *is*: a box (singular) of pencils *is* on the table. Similarly:

- 'the criteria (plural) *are*…'; 'the criterion (singular) *is*…'
- 'there are *fewer* (not *less*) rooms'
- 'it will be *more colder* tomorrow' (change to simply *colder*)
- 'the Queen Mother will *lay* [should be *lie*] in state for three days'.

Every language has its trickier aspects of usage and if you are not a native speaker of English, you may face problems of interference from your own language. For example, a Chinese student wrote: 'After briefly introduce the concept...' [should be *introducing*] and a German student wrote: 'not much people' when he should have written 'not many people'.

There are also differing attitudes to English usage, but if you are writing a formal report, you should not allow your poor or careless use of English to affect your argument. If you do so, you are less likely to communicate your message effectively to the people you are trying to persuade.

Should I use 'that' or 'which'?

Sometimes it is easier to remember a concrete example than an abstract rule, and here the words from the children's story 'The house that Jack built' are useful.

In 'The house that Jack built', the clause 'that Jack built' is *essential* to what you are trying to say. Let's call that a Type-1 clause.

In contrast, in 'The house, which was built by my grandmother, burnt down', the clause 'which was built by my grandmother' is *extra* to what you are trying to say. Let's call that a Type-2 clause.

In Type-1 clauses, we can use 'that' or 'which' and we put no comma, because a comma breaks things up and we want to get on to the essential information as quickly as possible. In Type-2 clauses, we can only use 'which' – 'that' would be wrong – and we put a comma at the beginning and end of the clause to show where it begins and ends: 'The house, which was built by my grandmother, burnt down.' Some people prefer to use 'that' for Type-1 clauses and 'which' for Type-2 clauses.

Write in paragraphs

Do you remember what a paragraph is? It's a unit of the text that consists of one major thought together with any explanation or illustrations connected with that thought. You should keep the topic clear throughout your paragraph.

This is where your earlier planning becomes important; hopefully you planned your text in paragraphs. However, if you did not, or the results of your planning are weak, you can revise your text so that the sentences in a paragraph all belong together and your argument flows well.

The most important part of your paragraph is the 'topic sentence', the key sentence of what the paragraph is about. It is usually, but not always, the first sentence in the paragraph.

So when I am writing, I constantly ask myself, 'What am I trying to say?'. As I noted yesterday, it can take time to refine precisely what you want to express. Once you are clear about what you want to express, write out the key thought and add further explanation or illustration for that paragraph.

Sometimes, you need to add an opening sentence so that readers can understand the context. For example, colleagues were writing a website about fishing and they had assumed that their readers knew all about the particular kind of fishing. When we discussed this, it became clear that what was missing was an opening definition of the particular kind of fishing they were writing about. You could ask yourself what the particular function of each sentence is: if you do this, you may discover that you have missed out steps in your argument. Or you may find you have repeated yourself, so you can put this right by shortening your text.

> **'I have written you a long letter because I have not had the time to write a short one.'**
> Blaise Pascal (1623-62), French philosopher, mathematician and physicist

Use linking words

We sometimes use linking words, or phrases, to show the direction of thought. Such expressions act as signposts to the direction in which we are turning the argument. Useful linking words include:

To introduce a contrast:

- Although...
- Despite this...
- However...
- In contrast...
- On the other hand...

To reinforce a point that you have just made:

- Besides...
- Furthermore...
- In addition...
- Moreover...

To show a result:

- As a result...
- Consequently...
- Therefore...

However, do not overuse these. We do not use such expressions in every sentence.

Write shorter sentences

The best average length for a sentence is 15 to 25 words. Of course, you can use shorter ones (like this). In particular, shorten very long sentences. If your first draft has too many clauses linked by 'and', split them up into different sentences.

Choose your words well

Have you used the word 'different' already? Change one of them (if appropriate) to 'various' or 'a range of'. Use a thesaurus. But be aware that very few words are completely interchangeable. A student wrote 'be obsessed with' whereas what she meant was 'be concerned with'.

Similarly, if you have used 'but' many times, you cannot simply change some of them to 'however' and think that is sufficient; you need to change the punctuation – and possibly the structure – of the sentence:

In modern usage many women dislike being addressed as 'Miss' or 'Mrs' because of the automatic assumption being made about their marital status. They are more likely to prefer the neutral 'Ms', *but* 'Ms' is disliked by some people because of its feminist associations.

'But' is too informal here; 'however' is more appropriate and more elegant. Note the punctuation and the position of 'however':

...They are more likely to prefer the neutral 'Ms'; however, 'Ms' is disliked by some people because of its feminist associations.

or:

...They are more likely to prefer the neutral 'Ms'. However, 'Ms' is disliked by some people because of its feminist associations.

or:

...They are more likely to prefer the neutral 'Ms'. 'Ms' is disliked by some people because of its feminist associations, however.

 TIP *Read your draft text out loud – you will be surprised at what you notice and want to change.*

Use fewer nouns and more verbs

We sometimes want to express the content of what we want to say as nouns, but the combination of a noun plus verb, or sharing the content load more with a verb, is more helpful. For example:

● 'The repercussions regarding the effects subsequent to the explosion will be perused by the managers' can be simplified to 'The managers will consider the effects of the explosion'.

- 'This article considers current monetary policy implementation procedures' can be changed to 'This article considers how the current monetary policy is implemented'.

Use more active, and fewer passive, verbs

In 'Caroline broke the window', *broke* is an active verb. We can also express the same meaning as 'The window was broken by Caroline', in which *was broken* is passive. Sentences that contain a passive verb are longer than those with an active verb. They are also more formal. Note that you do not need to express the person who performed the action. So, 'The window was broken' can stand by itself, as can 'The train has been delayed', which is useful when the announcer does not want to say who or what caused the delay.

However, sentences with passive verbs can be difficult to understand, mainly because they do not begin with a person.

So the example given earlier could be changed from 'This article considers how the current monetary policy is implemented' (passive) to 'This article considers how *finance ministers* implement current monetary policy' (active).

> **TIP** *Wherever possible, make people the subject of your sentence.*

Check your punctuation

Commas

We can highlight some of the most common errors here:
'Snow fell steadily throughout the night, in the morning the road was impassable.'
The comma is wrong here, because the sentence consists of two clauses (groups of words with a verb, the verbs being *fell* and *was*) that can stand by themselves, i.e. 'Snow fell steadily throughout the night' and 'In the morning the road was impassable' can each be sentences.

Solution: put a semi-colon between the two: 'Snow fell steadily throughout the night; in the morning the road was impassable.' (Alternatively, make the two clauses into separate sentences, or join the two clauses with 'and'.)

Here is another type of problem:

'When fiscal times are hard waste is a favourite target for politicians'

When you read this, your brain comes to 'hard waste' and stops to consider whether this is a common phrase or not.

When a dependent clause (one that cannot stand by itself) comes first in a sentence, we may need to add a comma to show where the dependent clause ends and where the independent clause begins, i.e. we need a comma after 'hard': 'When fiscal times are hard, waste is a favourite target for politicians' (*The Economist*, 29 January 2005, page 34). (If the clauses are reversed, the word 'when' marks the end of the independent clause and the beginning of the dependent one and so a comma is less necessary.)

Apostrophes

The apostrophe (') has two main uses:

● to show possession: my mother's phone, women's rights, many companies' websites, one year's experience, five years' experience
● to show that something is missing: It's (It is) raining; it's (it has) stopped snowing.

NB Using an apostrophe to show a plural is wrong: apples [*not* apple's] for sale, videos [*not* video's] to rent.

Check your spelling

You can use a spell-check to check your spelling, but it will not detect words that are spelt correctly but do not fit what you are trying to say (e.g. martial/marital; causal/casual). Further, be aware of words that you may easily confuse:

accept ('to receive')
except ('to exclude'; 'not including')

affect (*verb*) ('to influence or cause to change')
effect (*noun* or *verb*) ('a result'; 'to bring about or produce')

bought (past tense and past participle of *buy*)
brought (past tense and past participle of *bring*)

into ('entering to the inside of', e.g. he drove into the garage)
in to (*in* and *to* separately, e.g. she went in to buy a newspaper)

it's ('it is' or 'it has')
its ('belonging to it')

loose ('to release or unfasten'; 'not confined or tight')
lose ('to fail to keep or win')

principal ('most important'; 'headteacher'; 'sum of money invested')
principle ('a rule or standard')

stationary ('not moving')
stationery ('writing materials')

their (e.g. their books)
there (e.g. over there)
they're ('they are')

to (e.g. to go)
too ('also') (e.g. Can I come too?)
two (e.g. two eyes)

who's ('who is' or 'who has')
whose ('belonging to whom')

your ('belonging to you')
you're ('you are')

Certain words differ in their spelling in British and American usage:

practice (*noun*) (rugby practice)
practise (*verb*) (you must practise your batting more) (US: *practice*)

Some commonly misspelled words are:

accommodation	privilege
beautiful	seize
commitment	separate
disappoint	sergeant
exorbitant	supersede
hypocrisy	Wednesday

Watch the tone of your document

Certain words, for instance 'get' and 'do', are informal, so replace them in more formal writing; for 'get', use 'obtain' or 'become'; for 'do', use 'fulfil', 'prepare' or 'undertake'. There is a tendency to be too informal in more formal contexts. For example if you are describing the role of a project manager, you could say that the person needs to be able to 'keep many balls in the air' but such language would be inappropriate in a formal report which might instead say 'tackle a wide range of activities at the same time'.

On the other hand, do not write in a very formal style that you think will impress your readers.

So instead of	Write
ameliorate	improve
assist	help
commence	start/begin
necessitate	need
purchase	buy
terminate	stop/end
utilize	use

Don't be wordy; delete redundant words:

- in 'a free gift', *free* is redundant
- in 'for example ... , etc.', use either 'for example' or 'etc': you don't need both
- change 'in an accurate manner' to 'accurately'
- change 'at that point in time' to 'then'
- change 'going forward' to 'in the future'.

Avoid foreign words and phrases: change 'per annum' to 'yearly'; 'per se' to 'in itself'.

Avoid abbreviations that are not generally known and jargon and slang. Use expressions that your readers will be familiar with; or if you use more technical expressions, explain them.

Be consistent

For a long document, you should compile a list of your 'house style' to show your choice of variant forms, either of which is correct.

full stops with abbreviations	ie or i.e.
highlighting certain words	use *italics* or 'quotation marks'
hyphens	co-operate or cooperate e-mail or email
-*ize* or -*ise* on verbs	E.g. in 'organize' or 'organise' Note, however that certain -*ise* verbs cannot be spelt -*ize*, e.g. advertise, advise, chastise, circumcise, comprise, compromise, despise, devise, enfranchise, excise, exercise, franchise, improvise, merchandise, revise, supervise, surmise, surprise, televise.

numbers	E.g. up to ten written out; 11 and above as numerals
pronouns	'he', 'he or she' or 'they' in sentences such as 'Anyone can learn a foreign language if ___ want(s) to'
quotation marks	single '...' or double "..."
serial comma	in lists before 'and' and 'or': e.g. animals, such as cats, dogs and rabbits *or* animals such as cats, dogs, and rabbits
spellings	sizeable or sizable judgment or judgement
two words or one	headteacher or head teacher website or web site

Lists in bullet points

Consider whether the use of a list in bullet-point form is appropriate, especially for short phrases. People sometimes ask me about punctuation in bullet points: the trend these days is only to put punctuation (a full stop) at the end of the final point and not to have anything at the end of the other points in the list. If individual points consist of more than one sentence, think about whether the list should be presented in bullet points.

A more frequent mistake, however is that individual lines do not run on grammatically from the opening text, for example:

The successful candidate will be:
- skilled in numeracy and literacy
- able to speak at least two European languages
- have experience in using project-management software.

The error here is in the third bullet point, which does not follow on grammatically from the opening line, and should be changed to:

● experienced in using project-management software.

Summary

Today, you have read about checking your documents as we have continued to think about the general principles that underlie writing all documents. Our aim throughout today has been to check documents carefully so that their text is clear and expresses the message that you want to communicate. You have learned to:

make sure your text is accurate

make sure your text is grammatical

write sentences that flow in paragraphs

keep the topic clear throughout your paragraph

write shorter sentences

choose your words well

use fewer nouns and more verbs and more active, and fewer passive, verbs

check your punctuation and spelling

watch the tone of your document

be consistent.

SUNDAY

MONDAY

TUESDAY

WEDNESDAY

THURSDAY

FRIDAY

SATURDAY

Fact-check [answers at the back]

1. Revising my document after I have drafted it is:
a) helpful if you know what you are looking for ❑
b) nice if you like that kind of thing ❑
c) a waste of time ❑
d) an essential part of the writing process ❑

2. When I read through my text after I've written it, I discover that it isn't at all clear. So:
a) I send it anyway, hoping no one will read it ❑
b) I go home and ignore it the next day ❑
c) I spend time making the text clearer ❑
d) I send it, leaving the reader to work out what I wanted to say ❑

3. Checking that your facts are accurate and correct before you send off a document is:
a) unnecessary; no one bothers with that kind of thing ❑
b) what my boss does ❑
c) important if you have the time ❑
d) essential ❑

4. Which is correct?
a) There is much spaces in the new car park. ❑
b) There are less spaces in the new car park. ❑
c) There are fewer spaces in the new car park. ❑
d) There are less space in the new car park. ❑

5. In business writing, you should:
a) use more active and fewer passive verbs ❑
b) use more nouns ❑
c) use fewer active and more passive verbs ❑
d) I don't know the difference between active and passive ❑

6. Following the principles discussed today, which is correct and the clearest?
a) The exploration of the company strategy development process is discussed in this report. ❑
b) In this report we discuss a wide variety of the several different ways in which the company's strategy is developed. ❑
c) In this report we discuss a wide variety of different ways in which the company's strategy are developed. ❑
d) In this report we discuss a range of ways in which the company's strategy is developed. ❑

7. Which is correct?
a) The houseing market has been adversely affected by the recession. ❑
b) The housing market has been adversely affected by the recession. ❑
c) The housing market has been adversely effected by the recession. ❑
d) The houseing market has been adversely effected by the recession. ❑

8. Which is correct?
a) Look at the websites, which our company will design for you. ❏
b) Look at the websites that our company will design for you. ❏
c) Look at the websites, that our company will design for you. ❏
d) Look at the website's which our company will design for you. ❏

9. Which is correct?
a) Jack, can we help you too finish the article? Too of us want to help you too! ❏
b) Jack, can we help you too finish the article? To of us want to help you two! ❏
c) Jack, can we help you to finish the article? Two of us want to help you too! ❏
d) Jack, can we help you two finish the article? Too of us want to help you too! ❏

10. Which is correct?
a) The school wishes to appoint a new principle whose main task will be to raise standards. ❏
b) The school wishes to appoint a new principal whose main task will be to raise standards. ❏
c) The school wishes to appoint a new principle who's main task will be to raze standards. ❏
d) The school wishes to appoint a new principal who's main task will be to raise standards. ❏

Follow-up

1 Take a document (e.g. an email or report) that you have written recently.
2 Looking at the points given in the Summary above, which three points is your document strong at?
3 Looking at the points given in the Summary above, which three points is your document weak at?
4 What practical steps will you now follow to put right the three points you have identified as being weak?

MONDAY
SUNDAY
TUESDAY
WEDNESDAY
THURSDAY
FRIDAY
SATURDAY

TUESDAY

Write effective emails and reports

So far we've looked at the basics of the writing process: knowing your aims; thinking about and organizing your material; writing your first draft; and checking your document.

Over the remaining days of the week, we will look at writing specific kinds of document.

This is an important point: the kind of message you want to communicate will determine the way in which you communicate it. So you need to think about the best of way of communicating that message. Is email the best way? Or would a face-to-face meeting be better, e.g. to clarify misunderstanding? Don't neglect using the telephone: a phone conversation is very useful if you want to build a business relationship, negotiate a point, resolve a sensitive issue or want a verbal response that is not possible from written forms of communicating. You can always confirm what you have agreed in an email after your phone conversation. Or do you need to write a report or business proposal or plan to lay the foundation for what you want to communicate?

Today we will discuss:

writing emails

checking the tone of emails

writing letters

writing reports

writing business plans

Writing emails

Emails are great. We can communicate with colleagues all round the world instantly. But emails also have their disadvantages. We can receive too many unwanted ones that stop us getting on with the tasks we are supposed to be dealing with.

The key is to know the best way to communicate the main principle: email is not best for all situations.

We're back to our basic point in the Sunday chapter. Know your audience (A); know your intention/message (I); know what response you want from your audience (R).

Know someone's personal style: my boss, ten years older than me, prefers the phone; I prefer email.

Here are a few tips.

- Email is best for communicating short messages: giving information about meetings and asking for information or updates on progress. Send long material as an attachment, with the body of the email as a covering letter.
- Put a clear subject in the subject line (more than 'Hi Jane'). Being specific about your subject will help your reader know what the email is about. Change the subject line if the subject changes over the course of the email exchange.
- Use 'cc' ('carbon copy', from the days of paper) and 'bcc' ('blind carbon copy') sparingly. Only send copies to those who really need to see the email. To explain 'cc' and 'bcc': if I am emailing Colin and cc Derek and bcc Ed, then Colin will see I have copied the email to Derek but Colin will not see I have copied the email to Ed. ('bcc' can also be useful for bulk emails when you don't want individuals to know the identity of the people on your emailing list.)
- Unless you are writing to a close colleague, include some form of opening and closing greetings. The policy of your company and organization and your own personality will guide you to what is acceptable (e.g. I find 'Hi Martin' difficult to accept from someone I don't know at all). If in doubt, err on the formal side ('Dear Mr Manser') as you

can change from that formal greeting to the informal 'Dear Martin' and the even more informal 'Hi Martin', but you cannot change from the informal to the formal. General practice is that people quickly move to the informal, but I advise starting at the formal level if you are in doubt. Common standard closing greetings are: 'Kind regards' or 'Best wishes'.

- If you are writing a long email, put the key information at the beginning, so that it will be clear on the opening screenshot as your reader opens the email. Spend some time laying out your email. Group sentences in paragraphs that concern one subject. To highlight the response that you are asking for, repeat it at the end of your email.

- Watch the tone of your email to make sure it is not too abrupt. Consider adding softer opening and closing statements. Even a relatively harmless 'I look forward to hearing from you' could be misinterpreted under certain circumstances as 'Why are you late with this report?', so be careful. Such short phrases as 'Is that time convenient for you?', 'It seems that' or 'Thank you' can help soften the tone.

- Use only those abbreviations that are known to your readers.

- Do not type whole words in capital letters, which strongly suggest shouting.

- As part of your email 'signature' at the end of your email, also include other contact information, including your job title, phone numbers (landline, mobile) and postal address. Your reader might want to phone you to clarify a point.

- Remember that emails can be used as evidence in a law court so be careful about what you write on sensitive issues.

- If you're angry, draft an email but don't send it before you have calmed down and taken the opportunity to revise it.

- Don't forget that the guidelines on writing good English (in the Monday chapter) still apply. Email is not an excuse for careless punctuation or spelling. Check what you write.

- Use bullet points to express important information in lists, rather than as separate sentences in a paragraph.

Getting the tone right: an email chasing progress

Andy wants to get Anne to finish writing her report. She is already behindhand with it. Unfortunately, Anne is far closer to the detail than Andy so he doesn't want to alienate her, but instead he wants to motivate her to complete it as soon as possible. Here is an email, with notes, that Andy writes to encourage Anne to complete the writing as soon as possible. (The numbers in brackets refer to the notes at the end.)

Hi Anne,

I wonder how you are getting on with the Lauder report1(1). You will probably remember it was due a day or two ago(2). I remember how I spent ages on a similar report last year and always seemed to be two days from completing it: I kept on finding material I wanted to add, so I understand the situation you are in(3).

Do let me know if you have any particular difficulties that you want to discuss with me(4). Otherwise I hope to receive your report before too long(5).

Best wishes,

Andy

1 Far less direct than: 'Why are you late with...'.

2 Slightly vague; better than: 'You are three days late'.

3 Including this sentence shows sympathy and softens the 'why are you late?' aim of the email.

4 A further approach, opening the door to Anne if she wants to come back to Andy on specific problems.

5 Closing sentence. The final words 'before too long' are a softer version of 'in the near future'.

Writing letters

Although use of email is widespread, letters are useful for more formal statements and in certain situations, e.g. to express appreciation or thanks, to confirm the offer of a job, to provide a reference, or as a covering letter for formal submissions such as a proposal, a job application or a bid. Business letters follow certain conventions:

- include an opening greeting. If this is the first time you are writing to someone, use their title: Mr, Mrs, Ms, etc. If you know their first name, use that: 'Dear Freda'. You can also use the style of the person's first name and surname, especially if you are uncertain from the name (e.g. Sam, Jo, Chris) whether the recipient is male or female: 'Dear Sam Smith'. The styles 'Dear Sir' or 'Dear Sir or Madam' are very formal and more impersonal.
- include a closing greeting. If the opening greeting is 'Dear Freda', 'Dear Mrs Jones' or 'Dear Sam Smith', then the close is 'Yours sincerely' (capital 'Y' on 'Yours' and lower-case 's' on 'sincerely'). You can also add 'With best wishes' or 'Best wishes' before 'Yours sincerely'. If you have used 'Dear Sir' or 'Dear Sir or Madam', then the close is 'Yours faithfully' (capital 'Y' on 'Yours' and lower-case 'f' on 'faithfully').

Writing reports

The general advice already given about writing is important: know why you are writing the report, who will be reading it and how you will structure it.

Types of report include:

- a progress report
- a health and safety report
- an investigation into the causes of an accident
- a company report
- a feasibility report
- a legal report used as evidence.

Your audience may be colleagues, shareholders, a board of directors, a project board, a team of advisers or consultants, a committee or the users of a new product.

The purpose of your report may be to:

- examine whether a particular project, product, etc. is financially viable
- present a case for a decision on buying a product or service
- persuade someone to act in a certain way
- explain how a new product works
- describe the achievements, financial condition, etc. of a company
- inform colleagues of the progress of a project
- outline the cause of an accident or the nature of an incident.

Be clear about your audience, intention and response (see the Sunday chapter). Knowing these will determine, for example, how much information you should include in your reports. If in doubt, discuss with colleagues. In other words, don't agonize over writing ten pages when senior management only want one page. Moreover, your company or organization may already have a report template to give a structure to your report.

TIP *Ask a senior manager how long your report should be: don't agonize over writing ten pages when senior management only want one page.*

The content of reports

Reports normally have the following as a minimum:

- **Introduction**: providing the report's purpose, including its scope or terms of reference
- **Body of the report**: its main sections, outlining the procedure you have followed and findings, supported by statistics, facts and other information. You should distinguish such objective evidence from your interpretation of those facts in your argument.
- **Conclusions**: a clear summary that draws all your arguments together, and recommendations: the necessary actions arising from your conclusions that must be taken to implement the report's findings.

Reports are often structured with clear numbers and headings (e.g. 1, 1.1, 1.1.1, 1.1.2, 1.2) to help readers refer to different parts easily.

Depending on the length of the report, you may also include:

- an executive summary of the whole report. Such a summary should be able to stand by itself and be a concise statement of all the report's significant information
- appendices: a section at the end of the report that contains technical information that is too long or too detailed to be included in the body of the text
- bibliography: a list of references and other sources of information used and/or quoted in the report.

When presenting an argument in a report, bear in mind the following points:

- present facts clearly
- put forward arguments logically
- support your arguments with relevant quotations, easily comprehensible facts and examples (case studies)
- give reasons for and against a course of action
- keep to the main point at issue
- deal with significant assumptions.

Explanation and argument

Both explanations and arguments are used in communication, but it can be helpful to note the difference between them:

- an explanation answers the questions 'why' or 'how', by giving you the causes of something
- an argument tries to persuade you that a certain course of action is right or true by giving you reasons (evidence) for following it.

For example, a report into a railway accident at a level crossing will include an explanation as to why the accident happened. The report will also offer arguments that certain changes should be made to improve safety at the level crossing.

Writing persuasively

Report writing is not only about providing information. Remember that business is built on confidence and perception, so you need to be able to present facts in a convincing way.

Which inspires greater confidence: version A or version B?

A

Sales were awful for the first six weeks but picked up slightly in the final six weeks of Q3. Research and development were running away with spending far too much money so we had to cut their budget by half for the remainder of the financial year. We hope the economy picks up soon.

B

This report summarizes progress made in the third quarter. Business was initially slow but we are pleased to report that the last six weeks have seen an upturn in trading conditions and business improved significantly in the final month. We are therefore confident that we have now survived the most difficult period of the present economic downturn given the general economic conditions around the world.

We have also recently reviewed our procurement procedures and are confident that effective monitoring systems are now in place to keep costs under control.

Looking to the future, there are promising signs of a good forward-order book. We are in a strong position to take immediate advantage of any upturn that will come in general world trading conditions.

Clearly, B. Not only is the language in A too informal for a report, B is also far more positive, enthusiastic and inspiring in tone.

Writing a business plan

A business plan is a specific kind of report or proposal to obtain support, e.g. from a board of directors or a source of funding.

Here is an example of the structure of a business plan for a guesthouse in an Asian country.

Business Proposal

1 Introduction, background and vision
2 Aims
3 Market size; market growth; market gap
4 Target market
5 Location
6 Competition and positioning
7 SWOT analysis: strengths, weaknesses, opportunities, threats
8 Organizational structure, including skills of key personnel
9 Finance: costs, pricing of rooms, projected profits and breakeven point; funding streams; cash flow forecast
10 Activities planned
11 Unique selling propositions
12 Strategy: forming local partnerships (travel organizations, airline, taxi and bus operators); explore potential to link with other guesthouses to share services, buying power and to refer guests when full
13 Construction: when, how, why?

And an extract from Section 1.

1 Introduction, background and vision

The proposition is to establish a guesthouse in Thailand, catering specifically for backpackers.

Thailand has always been a popular tourist destination. There is an established infrastructure of travel and accommodation for the well-off traveller, but less so for those on lower budgets.

A gap in the market exists for those travelling independently but who are looking for more than basic accommodation. It is proposed to build a guesthouse that will offer backpackers a good standard of basic accommodation and facilities at rates that will be significantly lower than those charged by more well-equipped hotels.

This will be achieved by providing accommodation only, with no food facilities other than offering a simple breakfast. Thailand has a vast choice of food outlets at all levels, and backpackers tend to eat out locally, meeting others and sampling a wider range of traditional cuisine than could be provided by even the largest hotels. An accommodation-only guesthouse will be simple to build, will need to comply with fewer regulations and will require comparatively few staff, all resulting in a lower cost to the guest.

All the documentation required to support the proposal is provided, as detailed in the outline.

Summary

Today we have looked specifically at certain kinds of writing: emails, letters, reports and business plans.

It is important to communicate the right tone in an email or report. We have also noted that email is not always the best way to express your message.

SUNDAY

MONDAY

TUESDAY

WEDNESDAY

THURSDAY

FRIDAY

SATURDAY

Fact-check [answers at the back]

1. Email is the best way to communicate:
   a) never: I don't communicate with anyone anyway ❑
   b) occasionally, when I feel like it ❑
   c) always: that's the only way, isn't it? ❑
   d) often: I think about the best way to communicate my message ❑

2. Using the phone to build a business relationship is:
   a) a waste of time ❑
   b) very useful ❑
   c) too slow ❑
   d) inefficient ❑

3. When I write an email, I try to make the subject line:
   a) bold ❑
   b) vague ❑
   c) specific ❑
   d) obscure ❑

4. When I send an email, I send a copy to:
   a) everyone in my address book ❑
   b) my boss always, to protect myself ❑
   c) no one: I don't know how to do that ❑
   d) only those who need to see it ❑

5. Getting the tone right in an email is:
   a) a waste of time ❑
   b) a luxury if you have the time ❑
   c) important ❑
   d) unnecessary ❑

6. When writing a report:
   a) I don't bother structuring my material ❑
   b) I structure my material carefully ❑
   c) I ask someone else to structure it ❑
   d) my structure is so elaborate even I don't understand it ❑

7. When writing a report:
   a) I put all the material down, hoping that readers will be able to make sense of it ❑
   b) I carefully distinguish facts and interpretations ❑
   c) I put everything in lists of bullet points ❑
   d) I get so lost in writing that I don't really think about what I am writing ❑

8. When writing a report, I aim to be:
   a) clear, concise and logical in expressing my thoughts ❑
   b) home early to watch the football ❑
   c) as vague as possible to avoid committing myself ❑
   d) very obscure and complicated to stop the truth from being clear ❑

9. When writing a report I realize the need to:
   a) get all the facts down as quickly as possible ❑
   b) manipulate the facts ❑
   c) inspire confidence ❑
   d) be as informal as possible ❑

10. When preparing a business plan, I give:

a) an analysis of the different factors ❏

b) my gut feelings ❏

c) emotional generalizations not supported by firm evidence ❏

d) unrealistic expectations and assumptions ❏

Follow-up

1 Look at the last 20 emails you have sent. On reflection, do you think that email was the best form of communication for all of them? Which would have been better handled by a phone call or a face-to-face meeting?

2 Given your response to question 1, what will you now change for the future?

3 How will you write reports differently as a result of reading this book?

4 Look at an email that you have just written. Is its message clear? Is its tone appropriate? Is the action that you want the reader to take made clear?

5 Do you find writing persuasively comes easily to you? Why or why not?

SUNDAY

MONDAY

TUESDAY

WEDNESDAY

THURSDAY

FRIDAY

SATURDAY

WEDNESDAY

Give excellent presentations

So far we've looked at knowing our aims and starting to write and then revising your text as you edit it. On Tuesday, we considered writing effective emails, letters, reports and business plans. For the rest of this week, we continue to discuss particular kinds of writing, and today we come to presentations.

Think of the most memorable presentations you have ever heard. What marks them out? A clear structure? The speaker's content? His or her passion? Their visual aids?

The key to a successful presentation lies in the preparation: preparation of what you want to say and also of you as the speaker.

Today we will consider:

knowing your aims: your audience (A), your message or intention (I) and what response (R) you want from your audience

working out your key message and breaking that up into logical steps

deciding what visual aids will help communicate your message

knowing the importance of body language

preparing for feedback

Prepare thoroughly

'The key to a successful presentation lies in the preparation: preparation of what you want to say and also of you as the speaker.'

We're back again to our first point from the Sunday chapter. Think about the basics, i.e. AIR: know your audience (A), your intention (message) (I), and the response you want your listeners to make (R).

Audience: Who are your audience: senior managers? colleagues? colleagues from outside your company, some of whom might be critical?

How many will be in your audience: five, 50, 500? How much do they already know about what you are going to say? Will you need to sketch in some background? What are their thoughts and feelings towards you as speaker likely to be? Discover as much as you can about your audience before you plan your presentation.

Sometimes when I give a presentation, I actually think of one or two individuals who will be in the audience and on the basis of my knowledge of them prepare as if I am speaking only to them.

Intention (your message): Try to summarize your message in 12 words. For example, if I were speaking about the content of today's chapter in a presentation, the key message would be 'Prepare your presentation well; the way to a successful presentation lies in thorough preparation.'

Think about what you are going to say. Look back at the Sunday chapter on using a spider diagram and answering the question words *why, how, what, who, when, where* and *how much*. You may think it unnecessary to do this but doing so is often fruitful, because you are putting down your key thoughts before you begin to organize and order them.

Think about why you are giving the presentation. What is the context in which you have been asked to give it? Is there a hidden agenda?

Organize your thoughts. You are now in a position to put your thoughts and basic messages in a certain order.

You have worked out your key message – 'Prepare your presentation well' – and you can put the material in a certain order. Note that:

● you need to add an introduction and a conclusion: they are separate

● you should put your most important point first in the main part of your presentation

● the order of your draft may be different from the one you end up with. That is OK. It is only a draft. It is better to work on some order. For example, taking Sunday's spider diagram, add '3' in front of 'prepare useful visual aids' and add '5' in front of 'expect feedback'. I know that 'prepare useful visual aids' and 'expect feedback' are important but they are not the basic, primary aspects of what I am trying to say, so they can go later in the presentation. So a draft final order is as follows: (You can compare this with the final text.)

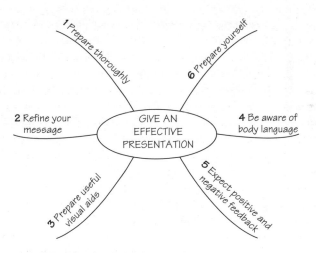

In the end, I put '6 prepare yourself' as a short paragraph – not as a main point – under '4 be aware of body language'.

Remember practical points.

Know how long you will speak for: 15 minutes? An hour? People will be grateful if you finish early (although not too early!) but will not appreciate it if you go on too long.

Consider the layout of the seating. If your style is interactive, then you will not want seating that looks too much like that of a classroom: a 'horseshoe' 'U' layout will facilitate interaction between the participants. Don't forget the room's lighting, heating or air conditioning.

Can't think of what to say?

Adam was a diligent worker but when asked to give a presentation on a subject he could only manage a few sentences and then he dried up, unable to think of what to say.

Fortunately, his friend George helped him and advised him to write out in advance the full text of what he was going to say. George even mentioned spider diagrams and the question words *who, why, when, where,* etc. to Adam. That careful preparation appealed to Adam and over time he mastered it and found he could expand what he was going to say on a subject. But he still found that he ran out of things to say. Again, George came to his aid, explaining that if, for example, his talk was to last for 30 minutes, he could speak for five minutes on each of six sub-topics (6 × 5 minutes = 30). Adam understood and accepted George's advice and over time became an accomplished speaker, able to speak for extended periods of time on a subject.

Refine your message

Work out your key messages. Be crystal clear about what you are trying to say. Keep your 'headlines' simple. Don't try to cram too much in – 'less is more'.

- Break down your key points into subpoints that support your one key point. Your key points should be clearly structured and ordered so that they flow naturally and logically from one another. Don't spend too much time on one point to the neglect of another. Work on your words. Use short, everyday words rather than longer ones. So use *try* rather than *endeavour*; *need*, not *necessitate*; *stop* or *end* rather than *terminate*; *harmful* rather than *detrimental*.

- Structure your main points in a logical sequence. If you can structure them by making them all start with the same letter of the alphabet or by using the 'ABC' approach (one of my talks on writing encourages writers to be 'accurate, brief, concise'), then your points will be more memorable.

- Say the same thing more than once. If your key point is 'Prepare well', then say that and add something like 'You need to work hard at the planning to make your presentation effective'. This is *expanding* on 'Prepare well', saying it again in different words. This is something you do more in speaking than in writing. You also do it in speaking when you see that your audience do not really understand what you are saying. This means you should look at them when you are speaking, not at your notes. Hopefully you are so familiar with what you want to say that you do not need to follow your script word for word.

- Think about how you will communicate. Ask questions. Give a specific example (case study) or tell a story to explain or support the point you are making. In this way, your presentation will be more memorable. Include some well-chosen quotations or statistics. Be creative. Find a picture that will illustrate the key point of your talk (but do bear in mind that you may need permission from the copyright holder to use the picture).

- Work on different parts of your presentation. Work especially hard on the *beginning*, so you capture your audience's attention and get them interested ('Did you know....? I was reading in today's newspaper...') and the *end* ('So the next step is...') to round off your presentation, drawing together and reinforcing application of your key points. Your task is to communicate to – and maybe challenge – members of your audience on the specific next steps that you want them to take.

● Check your message. This is important; check facts and dates to make sure they are accurate. A friend once mentioned the order of the planets in the solar system in a talk he was giving but unfortunately he named them in the wrong order, so the rest of his talk was less credible.

Think about your audience's response. In your preparation, continue to think about what the response of your audience is likely to be. Interested? Bored? In need of persuasion? Sceptical? Anticipate likely reactions by dealing with them in your preparation and in preparing answers to their questions.

Write your presentation down. Write down either:

1 every word you plan to say, or
2 notes that you can follow.

If you adopt the first method, then don't read it out word for word from your paper. Hopefully, your thoughts will have become part of your way of thinking. As you gain more experience, you will probably find you can work from notes. When I started giving presentations I wrote everything in pencil (so I could rub words out), then I typed them up (and enlarged the printout so that I could read it). Now, with more experience, I write out the key points, with important phrases or words highlighted. Do what you are comfortable with.

Be enthusiastic; be positive. You've a message to declare. Go for it! Think about your own approach to your talk. You have your own unique personality, skills and experiences. Be natural; be yourself. It took me years to discover and work out my own style for giving presentations. I was amazed when a colleague contacted me after a space of five years to ask me to lead a workshop at his company at which he said, 'I remember your style'. Be passionate. Your passion and enthusiasm (or lack of it) for your subject will shine through your presentation.

Do you remember a good teacher at school? I had one primary school teacher who was passionate about teaching us and my classmates and I still remember him (and his jokes) many years later.

Plan in a break. If your presentation is going to last longer than 45 minutes to an hour, then schedule a break so that your audience can relax for a few minutes.

Unseen, but important preparation

Hasheeb was wise. He'd given a few presentations and was beginning to enjoy them, even though he was always nervous before he gave one. He realized he would probably be giving presentations for several years, so he began to read more widely round the subject. He kept a hard-copy notebook and a computer file of useful ideas, stories, quotes and notes he came across. In this way, when he was asked to speak, he had a fresh resource he could refer to, so that his interest and passion remained fresh. This unseen, but important, preparation work was one of the secrets of his effectiveness as a speaker.

Prepare useful visual aids

Will you give handouts of your presentation? How many will you need? Work out when you will give them out: before or at the end of the presentation? My personal preference is before, so that the audience know where I am going. The disadvantage of this approach is that they do know where I am going, so always make sure that your notes are a skeleton (not the full text) of your presentation. Make enough copies of your handouts and some spare.

I made the mistake in one of my early presentations of preparing handouts that were in effect my full notes; so when a colleague said, 'We didn't need really to come, we could have just read your paper' I didn't have an answer, but I learned from that experience not to reveal my whole text on the handouts.

Use tables and charts to support your points, but don't be so complex or technical that your audience cannot understand what you are trying to say. Be as simple as you can be.

Also, consider using a model of something to communicate your point. For example, if you are describing the bad effects of smoking, a model that shows the effects of smoking on the lungs could have a great impact.

Use a flipchart if appropriate; I personally prefer a flipchart to a PowerPoint™ presentation as I find using a flipchart more flexible than the rigidly ordered PowerPoint. A flipchart allows the speaker to be audience-focused and respond to points raised in interaction with members of the audience.

If you are using PowerPoint, remember the following.

- PowerPoint is a means to an end, not an end in itself. Your PowerPoint slides should support your goal of communicating your message effectively, not be the goal itself.
- Allow plenty of time to prepare the presentation, particularly if you are not familiar with the presentation software. To begin with, it is likely to take far longer than you think.

- Don't try to put too much information on the slides. Keep to your headings, not complete sentences or the complete outline of your talk.
- Keep to one main font. Use a large font, ideally at least 28 pt. Aim to have no more than six lines on each slide. (Have you had the experience of peering over people's heads trying to read tiny print on a slide?) A sans serif font is easier to read than a serif one. Headings arranged left (not centre) are easier to read; capitals and lower case letters are also easier to read than text all in capitals.
- Check the spelling of words on your slides.
- Work out which colours work well, e.g. red on grey, yellow on blue.
- Use tables and charts to support your message; bar charts, pie charts, flow charts that give the key information visually work well. At one of my seminars, the pie chart illustrating that you should allow one-third of your time for research, one-third for writing and one-third for editing (as shown in the Sunday chapter) was one of the most memorable points of the whole seminar.
- Use illustrations that support your message, not ones that show off your design or animation skills (or lack of them!). Use short video clips (e.g. from YouTube). For example, if you are fund-raising and want donors to give to a particular project, seeing the plight of real individuals will demonstrate a situation and is more likely to stimulate the desired response than lists of statistics.
- Don't put the key information at the bottom of slides; people far away from the screen may not be able to see over the heads of other audience members.
- Rehearse the presentation with your notes/text in advance.
- Check whether you or a colleague will supply the projector, leads to connect the projector to your laptop and a screen. Arrive early to set everything up.
- Put your presentation on a memory stick (saved in earlier versions of PowerPoint for good measure) in case your laptop fails and you have to view it from someone else's laptop.

- Make sure that when you give your presentation your eye contact is with your audience, not with your laptop or the screen.
- Organize the room so that everyone can see the screen.

A picture is worth a thousand words

Jason was looking for suitable illustrations to accompany a talk he was giving on encouragement. He was emphasizing the 'tough but tender' aspect of encouragement and had a picture of a father and son to illustrate tenderness. He found it more difficult to find one for the tough aspect, however, until he remembered one of the tableaux in the Bayeux Tapestry in which a Bishop Odo was said to 'comfort' his troops by prodding them with a club. In modern colloquial English, he was 'giving them a kick up the backside' to goad them into action. The picture Jason found was a good illustration of the point he was trying to make.

Be aware of body language

A friend once told me, 'They are not listening to a message; they are listening to a messenger', so be yourself. Look smart and then you are more likely to feel smart and more confident. Dress professionally. A colleague and I once met a publisher to try to persuade them to take up the idea of a book we were working on. I was appalled when my colleague turned up in a sweatshirt and jeans – that wasn't the professional image I was trying to convey!

When giving your presentation, stand up straight and relax your shoulders. Don't hide behind the lectern (although I'm aware that positioning yourself there can hide your nervousness); you could even move around the room a little.

Maintain good eye contact with your audience – for me that is the critical point. If you are using a flipchart or PowerPoint, don't look at those while you are speaking; look at your audience. But look across your whole audience, not just at those you like. Remember too that your whole posture will reveal a lot about yourself.

Use your voice well – speak sometimes loudly, sometimes softly; sometimes faster, sometimes more slowly. Don't mumble; speak out clearly. Be expressive: vary the tone in which you speak. Use hand gestures, according to your personality. Smile (in my early days of giving presentations I went so far as to write the word 'Smile' on every page of my notes). Pauses can be useful to help your audience digest what you have just said.

Prepare your message so thoroughly that it becomes part of you. Practise it by speaking it out loud. This will also help you time it.

Prepare *yourself* as well as your *message*. The important point here is to be positive: you have been asked to give a presentation, so others have confidence in you. Be as enthusiastic as possible. Control your nerves. Take deep breaths. Drink water.

In your actual presentation, be authentic. Sometimes at the beginning of my workshops I sense that the participants and I are all nervous, so I will say, 'How are you feeling about today?', adding 'I'm as nervous as you.' Such genuine self-deprecating comments can help defuse their tension. Share something of your own personal approach to the subject as well as the standard material expected of you.

A difficult but good experience

Harry was keen to improve his presentation skills, so his colleagues recorded a presentation that Harry gave. Harry found that watching himself on video was a difficult but useful experience. He noticed mannerisms he was unaware of (jangling his keys), words he kept on repeating (his recurrent one was 'OK?'). But it was worth it. The awkwardness and embarrassment he felt were a necessary part of his own learning experience. Becoming aware of

his faults as others saw them was an important first step
to correcting them, as part of fulfilling his overall desire to
become an even more effective presenter.

Expect positive and negative feedback

'Feedback' means questions from your audience – and you
would be wise to prepare for them. These days many speakers
say at the beginning of a talk something like, 'I'll take any
requests for clarification during the talk but please keep any
more significant questions to the end.' If you say that, allow
time for both kinds of questions.

Here again, the key lies in good preparation. Expect
feedback. Expect a particular colleague to raise objections
because that's what he/she always does. Expect them ... and
plan for them. Deal with their objections and, where possible,
return to the key messages you want to communicate. (I
learned a trick here: when replying to an objector, don't keep
eye contact only with that person, but let your eyes roam more
widely through the room. If, while you give your answer, you
look only at the person raising the objection, then he/she may
take that as an opportunity to respond further.)

If you don't know the answer to a question, be honest
enough to say so. Often other colleagues in the room may be
able to help you out. Conclude a question and answer session
by again positively highlighting the key message(s) you want to
communicate to round off the whole presentation.

After your presentation, evaluate it. You could also ask
trusted colleagues to give their realistic assessment of your
performance. What was the content like? Was your delivery/
presentation too slow or too fast? Was it directed at the right
level? Did the handouts, visual aids or PowerPoint detract from
or add to your presentation? Recognize what worked well but
don't be afraid to acknowledge what didn't work well so that
you can learn lessons for the future. Remember: 'the person
who never made mistakes never made anything'.

How not to give a shared presentation

Colin and Peter were due to give a team presentation to secure funding for their new business. They knew their subject well and knew each other well too. Unfortunately, they did not think it necessary to work out in advance who was going to introduce the subject and who was going to speak about the details. So when it came to the actual presentation, Colin started to speak on the subject only to be interrupted by Peter. Both of them tried to answer each question and the whole presentation descended into chaos.

Needless to say, they did not secure the funding they were seeking: colleagues from the prospective funding agency would hardly make a substantial grant to such a seemingly unprofessional business as Colin and Peter represented.

Never again would they make such fools of themselves. In future, if Colin and Peter had to give a team presentation they would work out in detail in advance who was going to lead on each particular point, who would ask and who would answer questions, and who would bring the presentation to a close. They learned their lesson.

Summary

Today we've looked at giving presentations. We've seen that to give an effective presentation means that you need to prepare well. If you have prepared well, you are far more likely to be confident in delivering the presentation than if you have been careless in your preparation. Preparing well means that you will:

know who you are speaking to

know what you are trying to achieve by your talk

think about what you want to communicate

plan and organize your thoughts

work hard at the logical order and structure of your presentation

work hard at your words

work hard at your introduction and conclusion

prepare visual aids or PowerPoint slides that are as simple as possible

be aware of your body language as you deliver your talk. Be especially aware of keeping good eye contact with your whole audience.

SUNDAY

MONDAY

TUESDAY

WEDNESDAY

THURSDAY

FRIDAY

SATURDAY

Fact-check [answers at the back]

1. You've got to give a presentation in a week's time. Do you:
- **a)** prepare well? ❏
- **b)** panic? ❏
- **c)** get so nervous that you don't prepare at all? ❏
- **d)** not bother preparing, knowing you are good at improvising? ❏

2. What is the most important aspect about giving a presentation?
- **a)** working out what PowerPoint slides you can use ❏
- **b)** knowing how long you are to speak ❏
- **c)** knowing what the weather is like ❏
- **d)** knowing what your key message is ❏

3. When preparing what I am going to say:
- **a)** I jot down the first thing that comes into my mind ❏
- **b)** I take it slowly, thinking about my key message(s) ❏
- **c)** I don't prepare; I just improvise on the day ❏
- **d)** I spend all my time thinking but never write anything ❏

4. When giving a presentation, repeating what you say using different words is:
- **a)** useless repetition ❏
- **b)** useful to reinforce your message ❏
- **c)** nice if you have a wide vocabulary and thesaurus ❏
- **d)** a waste of time ❏

5. When constructing my argument:
- **a)** I carefully order the points I want to make ❏
- **b)** I don't bother organizing my points ❏
- **c)** I improvise ❏
- **d)** I lose the train of thought in my whole talk ❏

6. When I think about my conclusion:
- **a)** I just repeat my six main points ❏
- **b)** conclusion – what's that? ❏
- **c)** I round off my presentation with the next steps I want my audience to take ❏
- **d)** I add two new points to liven up my talk ❏

7. I use PowerPoint:
- **a)** always, as I want to show off my technical skills ❏
- **b)** never: I hate technology ❏
- **c)** usually, and put nearly all of my presentation on it ❏
- **d)** wisely, to support the points I want to make ❏

8. When giving my presentation:
- **a)** I keep my eyes on my notes ❏
- **b)** I look only at my colleagues ❏
- **c)** I look at the pretty girls in the room ❏
- **d)** I look at different members of the audience ❏

9. When speaking:

a) I vary the speed and volume of what I say ❏

b) I always speak in one tone ❏

c) I think I'm as bored as my audience ❏

d) I often use words such as 'um' and 'just' ❏

10. I expect feedback from my presentation:

a) rarely ❏

b) never ❏

c) often ❏

d) if I am lucky ❏

Follow-up

Think about a presentation you have to give in the next few weeks. Write out your key message in 12 words and the two or three subpoints that you want to make.

SUNDAY MONDAY TUESDAY WEDNESDAY THURSDAY FRIDAY SATURDAY

THURSDAY

Write persuasively

I regularly see three advertisements near where I live and work:

an advertisement for selling flats – with a picture not of an apartment but of a happy smiling couple

an advertisement for selling car-breakdown insurance – with a picture of a night-time, rainy motorway scene with the car bonnet up, and a cold and worried woman and child awaiting help

an advertisement for selling cars – with pictures of a car being driven along a bright forest road by a young man clearly enjoying his freedom.

What do all these have in common? They play on our emotions. They are not so much logical, reasoned ways of selling something but rather appeal to our natural human desires for happiness, security and freedom.

So today we move on from planning, editing and writing emails, reports and presentations. We change our focus to writing in a more persuasive style. Most writing is persuasive in some way – you're trying to influence someone to do something – but today is more directly concerned with this, in selling products or services.

Today we will consider copy writing, writing text for marketing, advertisements and press releases.

Customer-centred text

We're back to our first point in the Sunday chapter – the basics of communication: 'A' stands for 'audience'. When writing persuasively, you have to make your text reader-centred, targeted towards your customers. Here in particular we can see the need to understand who our intended audience is: and in addition to the basics of age, interests, etc. that we looked at earlier, we can add:

- what would your potential customers like to have more of in life; what is important to them, e.g. more money, more holidays, more clothes, opportunities, being more attractive; what are their values?
- what would your potential customers like to have less of in life, e.g. worry, stress, heavy weight, problems?
- how do your potential customers see themselves; how do others see them? How would they like others to see them, e.g. happy, secure, good-looking, important, better off than others?
- what is the unique selling proposition (USP) of your product or service: your unique promise to your customers?

... AS SOMEONE WHO FITS OUR TYPICAL CUSTOMER PROFILE, ...

Answering these questions will help you work out what you want your customers to feel. In the case of the advertisements mentioned at this chapter's opening, that would be:

● to feel happy and secure in a new home
● to feel safe and have peace of mind in their car
● to experience the freedom to drive where they want to.

So how do you get your customers to that point?

TIP *Knowing the unique selling proposition (USP) of your product or service is essential to successful marketing.*

AIDA

The memory prompt 'AIDA' has been used extensively and effectively to describe the different stages in moving a potential customer to take action, e.g. to buy a product:

Attention
Interest
Desire
Action

Attention

First of all, you must attract your potential customers' interest. You can do this in several ways.

Use a headline, especially one that focuses your readers' attention on the most significant benefit of your product or service. 'Update your wardrobe with...' (for the new season's fashion style), 'Learn in a week what the experts learn in a lifetime' (for the series of books that this title is part of, tapping into readers' thirst for and easy access to the knowledge of experts). Headings with 'how' work well:

● how to increase your profits by 20%
● how to cut your phone bill by at least 25%.

Remember that you're not giving an exhaustive description of everything in your headline; you're trying to attract your readers' attention and encourage them to read more, so:

- keep your headline short
- don't end your headline with a full stop, which would encourage your readers to stop reading further.

Use a question, especially open questions (i.e. ones with no fixed answer) or a closed question (i.e. one with the answer 'yes' or 'no') when you know the answer will not be 'no'. In asking a question, you must do all you can to avoid evoking the answer 'so what?'.

Use well-chosen pictures that attract your readers' attention.

Interest

Having gained your readers' attention, you then need to arouse their interest. You can do this by showing a need or arousing emotions.

Showing a need. The need may be obvious, e.g. to save money, lose weight, save time, become healthier, provide for your family if you should die, cure baldness or have more friends. If the need is not obvious, you need to show the readers why you think they need your product or service, e.g. to own a dream house or go on a dream holiday. Notice I said 'show'; you show your readers why you think they need your product or service. You don't tell them directly: you paint a picture that describes a scene so that they can visualize the scene and then conclude that they have a need (and that you have the solution to that need). Read the following:

'It's Monday morning ... 30 degrees ... you walk through the park sipping kumquat and lime juice: older folks dancing, a lady balancing several layers of wine glasses on her nose. Later, the lady moves on – and in her place, clowns perform in front of children – groups of deaf people sign to one another, many people walking, others exercising or doing tai chi ... this can be your experience on your dream holiday to China.'

It's evocative, isn't it, of a lovely scene that makes you want to book a holiday and leave the office immediately?

Arousing emotions. We have already mentioned this, but here you can think about possible emotional reasons why people buy certain products or services:

- to feel secure if the breadwinner in a family dies
- to remain healthy by eating certain products
- to be attractive to others by buying certain skincare products
- to feel important, or more important than others ('Buy our exclusive "Man Walks on Mars" T-shirt before we offer it to the crowd')
- to have more friends ('How to be liked by everyone')
- not to feel fear, e.g. a gym targeting its services at brides-to-be so that they will not feel afraid they are not going to fit into their wedding dress
- to be more successful ('The Ten Beliefs of Highly Successful People')
- to be happy with a new partner ('Find true happiness' – advertisement for a dating agency)
- to enjoy life more ('Take up Zumba in our gym').

You also have to respond to the possible objections your readers might bring up.

Desire

Having attracted your potential customers' attention and aroused their interest, you now want to stimulate their desire to buy your product or service.

There are several ways in which you can do this.

Introductory offers: 'Renewing your car insurance? Switch to us and we guarantee to beat your renewal quote by £25', 'Enter promotional code to save an extra 10%', money-off vouchers, free gifts, special offers, 'guarantees' to beat others' prices, all stimulate the customers' desire to spend their money on your product or service.

Motivating words: Did you notice 'guarantee' in the previous paragraph? It's a powerful word that makes you think that the company making such an offer is trustworthy. Other strong and positive words that will stimulate in customers a desire to buy, and help remove any obstacles that might restrain that desire, include the following:

best	'Probably the best you'll ever eat'
discount	'Buy now and we'll give you a 25% discount on your first order'
dynamic	'With our dynamic learning centre, you'll learn a new language in three easy steps'
easy	'Five easy ways to make money'
enjoy	'Order now and enjoy this sofa for Christmas'
exciting	'Get an exciting new job this year'
first	'Your first choice in buying new furniture'
free	'Starting a business? Enjoy up to £1,000 of free start-up benefits'
fresh	'We offer a fresh approach to building your website'
guarantee	'You can't lose with our money-back guarantee'
innovative	'Innovative output solutions'
key	'The seven keys to a successful CV'
new	'New year – time for a new you!'
now	'Order now and you will get a free phone'
only	'For one day only'
promise	'We promise to beat any other offer by 10%'
quick	'100 recipes for quick meals'

reliable	'The most reliable used-car brand'
save	'Save money now with our special offer'
special	'Special offer for one day only'
stylish	'Stylish cars for men'
taste	'Taste our delicious range of fresh food and wine'
tested	'Our tyres have been tested to the limit'
trust	'You can trust us – we've been in this business for over 30 years'
unique	'Our unique formula has helped thousands of asthma sufferers'
urgent	'Urgent: Offer must end Monday 9 p.m.'
win	'The best way to win sales'
you	'You know you deserve better'

Don't use too many of these words, however, or your writing will appear exaggerated, but equally don't ignore these words totally.

Other tips include:

Be brief: Many of the words in the table above are short one-syllable words. They work far better than their longer equivalents, so to increase sales, write 'now', not 'at the present time' or 'immediately'.

Be reader-centred: Note again, you must turn the focus away from yourself and concentrate on your customers. Keep asking the customer's question: 'What is in it for me?'

Which of the following is more effective?

A

As an energy company we know householders experience difficult times in the winter months and that is why we are introducing a new way to reduce bills.

B

One easy way to spend less on your heating bill this winter.

B, surely, is the one which is more customer-focused.

Use quotations: 'A clear, readable and reliable guide' was how the world-renowned theologian Alister McGrath described one of my books (*Crash Course on Christian Teaching* (1998) Hodder & Stoughton). I was flattered ... and his quotation helped boost sales, I am sure.

Use what well-known people and/or experts in their field have said about your products or services, with their permission. If you have undertaken surveys or questionnaires, use the responses and the findings from real customers in your copy. Such comments help instil confidence in your product or service and the perception that you are a trustworthy company or organization to deal with.

Use stories: Stories help create a link between your reader and you. Remember the story quoted above?

'It's Monday morning ... 30 degrees ... you walk through the park sipping kumquat and lime juice: older folks dancing, a lady balancing several layers of wine glasses on her nose. Later, the lady moves on – and in her place, clowns perform in front of children – groups of deaf people sign to one another, many people walking, others exercising or doing tai chi ... this can be your experience on your dream holiday to China.'

See how your interest is held and your emotions are evoked.

Stories can make your copy more exciting. Focus on details that your readers can easily associate with. On one of my courses a colleague was writing a press release about a multicultural festival. Frankly, the article seemed boring and written in a dry, unemotional way – exactly the opposite of the tone of the actual event. So I suggested that the writer focus on one Nigerian girl's involvement with the event – from her initial delight at being asked to participate through to the hard work of practice, fitting everything in with school homework and her mum taking her to the practice sessions twice a week. Then on the day of the actual event, her nervousness in the morning beforehand ... leading up to her thrill at eventually taking part in such an exciting and special celebration. The whole experience changed her life and reminded her of her Nigerian roots and identity. The words (and the writer) came alive as the writer discovered she could express herself differently.

Check your spellings: Don't spoil your press release or advertising copy by making elementary spelling mistakes. Check the spellings of people's names and their ages, if you include them in a press release: 'Charles Duckworth, aged 37,...' Your trustworthiness will be undermined if you get basic spelling wrong, e.g. if you confuse *it's* = 'it is' (*It's* a funny story) and *its* (Economic recovery will be on *its* way soon).

Action

This is the final step in AIDA; you have attracted your customers' attention, aroused their interest and stimulated their desire to buy. You now want to move them to action and to actually buy your product or service.

Repeat the benefits: You know what the benefits of your product or service are, but include them again in summary form, e.g. just before your call to action, as clear facts in bullet points.

Make it easy: Some sales letters I receive make my possible response very complicated (e.g. I have to fill out my details of name, address, etc. when the company already has these); the other ones I'm more likely to respond to make it easy – with a tear-off slip with my details already printed on it, and enclosing a reply-paid envelope so I don't have to try and see if I have a stamp. Similarly, some websites seem to invite easy-to-make responses, while on others you have to search for a long time to find the 'Contact us' page and then you have to fill out many boxes to complete the online form.

Be clear: Make it unambiguously clear what the next step is for your customers. So if you are a hotel, make sure you include on your website a map and directions as to how to get to your hotel and where your car park is located.

If you're writing a sales letter, make sure all your contact details, including all mobile numbers, are clearly shown – you don't want your customers to be put onto voicemail just when they want to take action. Include:

- a phone number or an email address to respond to
- other contact details
- an order form that is easy to fill in

- a call to action, preferably with an additional incentive ('Order by 31 May and you'll get an extra 10% off').

A great team

Mike was part of a great team. He was a skilled copywriter but not a designer. Fortunately his colleague Steve was a designer so together they worked well: Mike writing the words, Steve presenting them most effectively. Steve was particularly competent at producing a well-designed layout with good use of typefaces, wise use of emphasis (capitals, bold, italics, colour: not too much and not too little), bold captions and carefully chosen illustrations. Steve was particularly keen on ragged right (unjustified right) text to give more space, so that his documents were easier to read than if the text was justified (flush) left and right. Together they worked on subheadings that used certain key phrases of the text and kept the readers' attention. Making the most of their skills, Mike and Steve were well known for developing effective advertisements that were not only informative and attractive but also generated increased sales.

Writing a press release

A press release is focused at a specific audience (generally journalists), and is designed to convince them that your copy is interesting enough to be included in their publication (or website, blog, etc.) and therefore give your product, event, etc. a much wider audience and an authorial stamp of approval. A successful press release is one which a journalist can print verbatim.

The elements to use in structuring a press release are the answers to the question words we considered in the Sunday chapter: *who*, *what*, *where*, *when* and *why*, i.e. the same as a journalist would use in reporting a story.

In a press release, the emphasis on direct selling is reduced – the press release isn't making a direct appeal to the customer, but by giving a certain amount of information in a persuasive format, is drawing attention to the sales proposition and encouraging the reader to look into it further. The 'doing' section at the end (for further information ... contact ...; see website, etc.) is just as relevant as for sales copy. The 'story' element is also important, and using examples to bring the piece to life is always useful.

Sample press release

Gala reopening for The Hollies Hotel

After seven months of major refurbishment, The Hollies Hotel in Seabrook was declared open today by local celebrity chef Seamus Logan. The hotel has been the subject of a major overhaul, transforming it into a sumptuous country house and spa destination.

The McDougall family have owned the hotel for over 50 years and Jim McDougall, the current owner, said: 'We are absolutely delighted with the results of our refurbishment programme. We have spent nearly half a million pounds upgrading the hotel so that it is fit for the 21st century. The Hollies has always been a warm and friendly establishment, but now we can offer all the latest luxuries that visitors increasingly expect.'

As well as all bedrooms, bathrooms and reception rooms receiving a makeover, there is also a brand new spa with fully equipped gym, sauna, treatment rooms and heated swimming pool.

The restaurant has also received special attention and boasts a delicious new menu to suit its updated look. Celebrity chef Seamus Logan said: 'I would be proud to call any of these dishes mine – the kitchen team here are doing an excellent job.'

The hotel, spa and restaurant are now open for bookings.

ENDS

For further information, contact:

Emma Smith on xxxxxxx or email emma@xxxxxx

Summary

Today we've focused on writing persuasively in order to move your potential customers from not being particularly interested to actually spending their money. We've concentrated on:

getting to know your potential customers even more, especially their beliefs, values, wishes, attitudes and feelings

emotional factors and making sure that your whole approach – pictures and well-chosen words, design and layout – all work together to produce the desired results

the memory prompt 'AIDA' (attention, interest, desire, action) to move your potential customers to make a purchase.

SUNDAY
MONDAY
TUESDAY
WEDNESDAY
THURSDAY
FRIDAY
SATURDAY

Fact-check [answers at the back]

1. In writing advertising copy, you should put the focus on:
   a) nothing in particular ❑
   b) your potential customers ❑
   c) yourself ❑
   d) what you are going to eat for lunch ❑

2. Knowing your unique selling proposition (USP) is:
   a) a waste of time ❑
   b) a nice-to-have ❑
   c) essential ❑
   d) a luxury ❑

3. The memory prompt 'AIDA' stands for:
   a) advertising, intention, demonstration, action ❑
   b) accountancy, information, decision, authority ❑
   c) assumptions, internet, diversity, action ❑
   d) attention, interest, desire, action ❑

4. Persuasive writing in an advertisement should:
   a) use many short one-syllable words to be direct ❑
   b) use lots of long words to impress your customers ❑
   c) use a wide range of styles to reach different audiences ❑
   d) be what comes into my head ❑

5. Showing your potential customers an idea rather than telling them it directly:
   a) is a waste of time: I prefer to go immediately to telling them ❑
   b) is helpful if you know what 'show, not tell' means ❑
   c) is so difficult that I give up ❑
   d) allows customers to visualize a picture in their mind ❑

6. Arousing your potential customers' emotions is:
   a) always wrong because it is manipulative ❑
   b) an effective part of advertising and marketing ❑
   c) nice to have if you know who your customers are ❑
   d) ineffective: you must appeal directly to their minds ❑

7 In helping to stimulate your potential customers' desire, using quotations from satisfied customers and stories is:
   a) not possible: we've not got any satisfied customers ❑
   b) futile ❑
   c) very useful ❑
   d) just about valid ❑

8. When I have finished writing a press release:
   a) I check that the spellings and contact details are correct ❑
   b) I hope for the best even though I know my spelling is bad ❑
   c) I don't have time to check anything ❑
   d) Finish? I'm a perfectionist so never complete anything ❑

9. How do you encourage potential customers to act and buy your product or service?
a) I've never really thought about it. ❏
b) We don't have any customers. ❏
c) We make it as easy as possible for them to order goods online. ❏
d) We make it as hard as possible so that we are not bothered by customers' enquiries. ❏

10. The design and layout of an advertisement are:
a) irrelevant ❏
b) as important as the words ❏
c) far less important than the words ❏
d) not something I've ever thought about ❏

Follow-up

1 List six beliefs, values, wishes, attitudes or feelings of your potential customers.
2 Consider 'AIDA' (attention, interest, desire, action): which of these is your company or organization particularly strong at? Which is your company or organization particularly weak at? What practical steps can you take to correct this weakness?
3 What is your unique selling proposition (USP)?
4 Write a sample advertisement for your product or service, incorporating what you have learned today.
5 Write a sample press release for your company or organization. What story can you focus on?

FRIDAY

Build a successful website

Your website may be the 'shop window' of your company or organization, but what exactly do you mean by that? You may want to promote your services or products, or an author or a rock band. You may want to inspire users by your choice of photographs or stories. You may want to inform or educate users about a particular need and maybe ask them to give money towards your cause. You may want to alert important people in your industry, but not want to attract detailed queries from individual consumers that will be time-consuming to deal with. Or you may want individual customers to purchase direct from your website.

Websites have become such an essential part of business life that it is difficult to imagine life without them. Yet we are also aware that some websites are easier to navigate than others and information is more accessible on some than on others. So today we will consider:

knowing your aims and planning your website carefully, so that the information is organized in a way that is accessible to the users you want to target

writing text for your website, with tips on design and the layout of your words and pages, to ensure that your website is as effective as possible.

Know your aims

As I have mentioned in earlier chapters, it is essential that you clarify the exact aims of your document, and this also applies to your website. You need to know:

- who you are aiming at (A: audience)
- what you want to communicate (I: intention or message)
- what response you want (R: response).

Underlying all these is the need to clarify precisely what the purpose of your website is.

So what do you want your website to do? Your website may show the location of your office or store, and your opening hours. The website may show your goods or services, but do you want customers to buy direct from you or via a retailer or other intermediary? How do you want interested users of your website to respond to you? If you are offering a service, and if users want to complain, do you want to make it easy or more difficult for them to do so?

Plan your website

When you are clear on the aims of your website, you can plan it.

Work out your users' needs. What are they? To know the aims of your company or organization? To be persuaded they need to buy your product or service or donate money? One way of beginning to think about this is to write a brief mission statement. You can fill this out with longer explanatory paragraphs and case studies (real-life examples) of your company or organization at work.

Think hard about how and when your users will use your website and what information they want. For example, my wife and I recently renovated our bathroom and when we were planning the renovation, we accessed different companies' websites for details of the tiles, baths, basins, etc. they offer. Some companies gave prices on the website, some in a separate downloadable brochure; some didn't give prices at all!

Some users will view your website for only a few moments; others want to read what you have to say and respond positively, for example by buying a product or finding the information they want. Do you want users to download further files (e.g. in pdf format)? How do you want users to contact you? Think it through as practically and as realistically as possible.

Organize your website

Here are some tips.

- Plan a hierarchy of information, i.e. how you want users to go from one page to the next.
- Remember that people will navigate your site in a variety of ways.
- Separate your information into major – but manageable – parts. Group such parts into categories.
- Plan from 'the bottom up' – start with your most detailed pages and work backwards to your home page.
- Allow for flexibility. For example, if you are selling ebooks in various formats, allow for further tabs to be added on your website alongside your existing ones in anticipation of future changes in technology.
- Imagine a user accessing your website and work through how they will navigate your site. Make sure that the choices you are offering are the ones you want to offer. Some websites are built on the 'three-click' principle: give users the information they want within three clicks from the home

page or they will go elsewhere. But in reality, if users are interested – and determined – enough, they will pursue your website more deeply.

● Have a balanced combination of words and images. Some websites seem to contain only words; some only images. I think an effective website will contain both, to reflect the fact that some people learn from words, while others find visual elements (photographs, illustrations, graphics, diagrams, etc.) more helpful. You could also consider including a short video, or a YouTube link, to explain, for example, how one organization benefited from using your company's services.

● Give constant calls to action, e.g. 'Buy now', 'Contact us', to make it as easy as possible for your users to make the response you want.

● Consider specifically Search Engine Optimization (SEO), i.e. how you will reach your target audience most effectively through the use of keywords (search words) in your text and its title.

● Plan how you will maintain your website. It is fine to work very hard on your website now, making it active by a certain date, but you also need to plan how you will keep it up to date. Too many websites have a 'latest news' section with stories that happened a year ago or more. Having out-of-date information does not communicate an image that your company or organization is successful *now*. So the rule is: make intentional plans to keep your website fresh.

SUNDAY
MONDAY
TUESDAY
WEDNESDAY
THURSDAY
FRIDAY
SATURDAY

TIP Plan how you will maintain your website and keep it fresh. Make sure your 'latest news' is not out of date.

A new concept

Ray, one of the directors of the plumbers Smithson and Son, asked Jo, a website consultant, to design and build their company's website. When Jo first met Ray, she explained that a website was different from the normal printed pages of a book, in that a website does not really have a finishing point; it is much more flexible than the traditional printed page. Pages on a website are more like photographs: they provide a visual snapshot for users. The interactive nature of websites was an entirely new concept to Ray. Previously, he thought he could just put his company's existing leaflets on the website by cutting and pasting the text and that was all that was needed. Jo helped Ray see that the company's website could open up a whole new world, enabling customers to see what the company offered.

Write your website

Here are some useful tips.

- Keep your users' needs constantly in mind. You are writing for them, not for yourself. Writing for a website is like having a conversation, except you cannot see the person you are talking to.
- Make sure your home page says:
  - who you are and your basic aims
  - the goods and/or services you offer
  - how users may obtain your goods and/or services.
- Make your text easy to read. Good practice has shown:
  - it is best not to put text right across the full width of the screen; if you do so, the text will not be legible. It is better to use up to half the width of the screen

- the best position is towards the top of the screen and towards the left
- text that is centred on the page is difficult to read, so align your text – including headings – to the left, but keep the right-hand side 'ragged' (unjustified)
- a sans-serif font is more legible than a serif one on a computer screen
- you should keep the colours of your text and background different, but don't use too many colours.
- Give each page its own title.
- Divide your text into paragraphs and write a clear heading above the paragraph. Keep paragraphs to no more than 100 words.
- Have white space around your text: this creates an impression of openness.
- Put the most important information first in each paragraph.
- Keep your sentences short: a maximum of 15–20 words.
- Use everyday words that you would say in a normal conversation, e.g. *explain*, not *elucidate*; *more* or *extra*, not *supplementary*.
- Be direct; use 'we' and 'you' rather than 'the Association' and 'consumers'.
- Make sure your text is clear. Draft the text and then revise it: look back at the Monday chapter on editing your text.
- Add hyperlinks to other pages on your website and/or back to your home page; e.g. Click <u>here</u> to find out more or <u>contact us</u>. (When users click on the underlined words they will be taken to a new page or a form.) Excessive use of hyperlinks can, however, make the page look too detailed.
- Make sure your spelling is correct: 'Philips' or 'Phillips'? Be consistent (e.g. use *-ise* or *-ize* throughout). Incorrect punctuation will undermine your website's accuracy.
- Keep punctuation to a minimum; full stops at the ends of bullet points can make a website look fussy.
- Avoid abbreviations that are not generally known, and jargon and slang.
- Put information in lists, which work well on websites.
- Make sure your text is accurate. Check dates and financial information so that they are correct.

Summary

Today we've looked at building a successful website: how to know your aims and moving on from those to planning and organizing your website so that it fulfils those aims. We have then looked at different aspects of writing for your website to make sure your message is communicated successfully.

SUNDAY

MONDAY

TUESDAY

WEDNESDAY

THURSDAY

FRIDAY

SATURDAY

Fact-check [answers at the back]

1. My website is:
   a) a luxury ❑
   b) a waste of time and money ❑
   c) essential ❑
   d) nice to have when I can afford it ❑

2. Your website is:
   a) your organization's shop window ❑
   b) your organization's rubbish tip ❑
   c) a set of printed leaflets just put onto the web ❑
   d) the IT department's responsibility ❑

3. The first thing to do when planning a website is:
   a) start writing as soon as possible ❑
   b) organize the pages ❑
   c) be flexible ❑
   d) know your aims ❑

4. When designing web pages, put text in:
   a) more than the width of the screen ❑
   b) up to half the width of the screen ❑
   c) the whole width of the screen ❑
   d) we'll set up a committee to discuss this ❑

5. Working out how users will navigate the website is:
   a) a luxury ❑
   b) essential ❑
   c) a waste of time ❑
   d) important if you have the money ❑

6. When designing web pages, you should:
   a) use a sans serif font and lots of headings ❑
   b) use a serif font and lots of headings ❑
   c) use a serif font and no headings ❑
   d) use a sans serif font and no headings ❑

7. Giving each page a title is:
   a) unnecessary; users can see what it's about ❑
   b) a nice idea if you are creative ❑
   c) important; do it ❑
   d) extravagant; it takes up too much space ❑

8. We need to update our website:
   a) regularly ❑
   b) never ❑
   c) when we have time ❑
   d) if customers tell us it's out of date ❑

9. When building a website, you should think about:
   a) using only text; those who like pictures must accept you're not providing any ❑
   b) using only pictures; those who want text must accept you're not giving them that ❑
   c) using a mixture of text, graphics and videos with your target users constantly in mind ❑
   d) just importing the company brochures and hoping for the best ❑

10. After writing text for the website:
a) the website goes live immediately ❏
b) if I have time, a colleague may check it ❏
c) the website goes down; what did I do wrong? ❏
d) check the text to make sure it is clear and accurate ❏

Follow-up

Be brave: monitor your website. Look at it with fresh eyes, with the eyes of one of your intended users. Ask yourself certain basic questions:

1 What are its aims? Who is it directed towards?
2 Does it achieve its aims? What objective evidence do you have for your answer?
3 Are the current aims of your company or organization reflected in your website or have you moved on from when the website was originally built?
4 Could you add some brief video clips to support your key messages?
5 What effects do the visual elements, e.g. pictures or videos (or lack of them), choice of font, amount of white space (or lack of it) convey about your overall message?
6 Is your website updated regularly?

SATURDAY

Use social media effectively

As the pace of innovation in the Internet age has quickened, use of social media sites such as Facebook has become an important part of many people's lives. The impact of these sites is still being assessed but undoubtedly digital formats will remain immensely significant for the foreseeable future.

The number of interactive networking websites is changing constantly; we will consider LinkedIn and Facebook especially, but the principles discussed can be applied elsewhere. We will also consider blogs and Twitter.

Professional networking sites such as LinkedIn allow you to keep informed about trends in your area of business, network with colleagues around the world, discuss matters of common interest and see what business opportunities may arise.

Blogs and Twitter help you to develop an online community by connecting with potential and existing clients, sharing links to interesting articles, exchanging pictures, information and specific insights, discussing ideas, and asking – and responding to – questions.

So how can you harness different Internet social media possibilities effectively to develop business relationships with your target audience and increase your business? What are their potential uses in a business setting?

Getting started

Before we look at different social media, here are some general guidelines.

- See social media as an important part (but not the only part) of your marketing strategy.
- Know your aims. As we have said several times in this book already, work out your aims:
  - do you want to develop more contacts? Then, for example, LinkedIn is excellent.
  - do you want to get a following? Then Twitter may be more suitable.
  - do you want to market your product or service? Then perhaps Facebook would be most appropriate.
  - do you want immediate feedback from your consumers or end users? Then you might find Twitter the most helpful.
  - do you want to keep your end users engaged and in touch, for example with changes to your service (e.g. delays)? Then Twitter or Facebook could well help.
  - do you want to share your creative ideas, keep your present customers and explain new products? Then a blog might be most helpful.
  - do you want to strengthen a community? Then Facebook might well help.
- Know your audience. Who are they? Don't write a technical blog if you're writing for non-professionals.
- Keep your writing reader-centred. We're back to thinking through the benefits for your readers/users, not simply the features that you want to mention. The great difference in social media is that online social media have shifted power from producers to consumers.
- Keep your writing simple and concise. Clearly, the limit of 140 characters in Twitter forces you to do that in that medium.
- Keep listening. What are readers/users really saying? Direct your message at *their* level, not yours.
- Keep your writing in tune with your aims. For example, if you're a musician, your tone will be conversational; if you're an architect a more authoritative tone would be appropriate.

- Keep your writing grammatical. Using social media isn't an excuse for careless grammar or spelling.
- Join a group – engage in discussion; swap photos, ideas, etc. Hopefully the group's members will have a wide range of skills and knowledge and can bring not only their advice and experience but also their hopes and creative ideas for the issues that are being discussed.
- Keep your content up to date. Once you have decided on your aims, you can work out how much time you want to invest in social media. If you are writing a blog, then posting new material once a week is worth aiming at. Try to remain fresh, strong and innovative, whether you are writing your own blog or posting on blogs other than your own.
- On business sites, be professional. On all sites, be polite; don't share private or personal matters or material that could be considered morally offensive. Don't do things that will compromise your integrity.
- Be yourself – don't pretend to be someone you're not.
- Remember these sites are public, not private. It's like being in a railway carriage and speaking on the phone – everyone can hear what you are saying.
- Add links. In the old days of writing reference books, we added cross-references to related material: 'See also...'. Provide further sites for your users to pursue.
- List your blog, Facebook, etc. accounts as part of your email 'signature' and with your website address.

TIP *See social media as an important part – but not the only part – of your marketing strategy.*

LinkedIn

LinkedIn is a website on which you can see your contacts and then view who they know and see who you in turn are connected to. Connections are important to LinkedIn: it works on the basis that business opportunities come about by networking. Many people join LinkedIn because they have received an invitation by email.

Here are some tips on making the best use of LinkedIn.

- Spend time writing your profile. What makes you unique? If you find this difficult, imagine you are writing about someone else. Present yourself well, with your skills, background, experience and professional achievements.
- Include a photograph of yourself: spend time making sure you choose one you are happy with.
- If you're a company, follow the instructions at the 'Companies' tab.
- Keep your profile up to date by adding new material.
- Invite other people, e.g. business contacts, former colleagues and people you have worked with in the past (who you may have lost touch with) rather than those you don't know at all. Write a specially worded message to specific people, rather than sending out a general message to all.
- Obtain background information on potential colleagues, which is very helpful if you want to recruit someone.
- Recommend and endorse your contacts.
- Join discussion groups that are relevant to your areas of interest or expertise. Contribute from your experience. Ask questions. Be connected. You may find you gain a strong reputation for answering questions and are perceived as being well-informed on key issues.
- Follow up further leads and remain in touch with colleagues and networking contacts.

Facebook

Facebook is more social and personal than LinkedIn – here you can describe more of your personality, hobbies and interests.

- Create a group, invite friends and start sharing. When the group is set up, you can add updates and share with everyone in the group at the same time.
- Be friendly and conversational in tone.
- Post photos and videos; ask questions, e.g. 'Who can help with the jumble sale on Saturday?' or 'I've got a spare ticket to the Take That concert/football game on Wednesday. Would anyone like it?'
- If as a business you want to set up a page on Facebook:
  - choose the appropriate business category
  - add a photograph, logo or image as part of your profile
  - describe your business concisely
  - include your web address
  - invite others.
- Businesses can pay for advertisements that target particular groups by age, location, gender and interest, e.g. you can reach an audience in your city.
- Keep creating posts as part of Facebook's 'News Feed', the central column of the home page that is continually updated by the stories from the people and pages you follow. Make sure the content is relevant; reach your customers with a special offer (look back at the Thursday chapter), e.g. '25% off all coffee till Monday'.
- Plan ahead – it's no use posting special Christmas deals on 22 December; they should have been thought about months or weeks earlier.

Blogging

Think of a subject that is close to your heart: your thoughts about life, ways to bring up toddlers, your favourite new recipes, or how to expand your business. Choose something you feel passionate about because you will need to write about it regularly – and you don't want to run out of material after a few weeks.

Other points to consider:

- What is your unique approach to a subject?
- What are your basic aims?
  - who are you writing to (A: audience)

- what kinds of thing do you want to share? (I: intention or message)
- what do you want your readers to do with the information on your blog when they have read it? Think through all these things as they will shape what you write (and what you don't write) and how you write it. (R: response)

● Do you want to pass on your knowledge and skills to others? Do you want to update your friends or colleagues on your latest experiences? Do you want to help and inspire others?

● Think of a catchy name for your blog; undertake research that will help people find your blog.

● Decide who will host your blog, e.g. Blogger, WordPress.

● Decide whether you want your blog to be private (e.g. just for friends and family) or open to all.

● Add something about yourself.

● Start writing! There's plenty of information earlier in this book to help you work out how to think, plan, write and edit your text. Keep your blogs fresh and innovative.

● Write with sensitivity about private or political issues.

● Write strong headlines. Avoid careless grammatical mistakes. Add links to websites, articles, etc. that might interest your readers.

● Use other social media (e.g. Facebook, Twitter) to connect people to your blog. Link your blog to your website.

Fiesta Movement by Ford

Probably one of the very first and most successful social media marketing campaigns was launched by Ford in April 2009. It was called the Fiesta Movement. The tactic that Ford used was very innovative... What they did was loan a Ford Fiesta to 100 of the top bloggers to use for six months. In exchange, all that Ford asked of the bloggers was to upload a video to YouTube about the Fiesta and post an independent account of their experience with the car on their respective blogs.

The campaign was a massive success. There were more than 700 videos created by the bloggers, which generated over 6 million views on YouTube (this is a major amount as the average video only gets 100 views), more than 3 million Twitter impressions and Flickr was flooded with more than 670,000 photos of the Ford Fiesta. There was so much buzz created about this vehicle that 50,000 consumers in the United States alone wanted more information about the Ford Fiesta and a whopping 90 per cent of them had never owned a Ford before.

In the first six days, Ford sold 10,000 Ford Fiestas (meaning they made millions...).

Ford didn't stop there. The success drove Ford ... to look even closer at social media. They went looking for actual feedback from consumers. They went to sites such as www.SyncMyRide.com (a forum site where owners of cars talk to one another), which had logged a number of complaints about the automated voice on the Ford SYNC system. This information helped Ford make improvements to the quality of the voice.

So all in all, Ford used forums, Flickr, YouTube and blogs to implement an incredibly successful social media marketing campaign.

From Nick Smith, *Teach Yourself Successful Social Media Marketing In A Week* (2013) Teach Yourself

YOU SHOULD TRY IT — IT'S GREAT!

Twitter

Twitter is a network that consists of 'tweets', messages of up to 140 characters, where users find the latest news on certain events.

You can use Twitter to:

- share news of the latest updates, events and the current progress of projects
- ask for feedback from your followers
- give advice; ask for others' opinions
- provide your followers with special offers or discounts
- provide links to related blogs, websites, etc.
- forward tweets posted by your followers
- write in a personal, direct way not only about what you are doing but also about what attracts your attention.

Remember: you don't have to read every tweet or reply to every tweet.

Two terms:

- a 'trending topic' is one that is worked out as being currently popular and of interest to you
- a 'hashtag' (#) marks keywords or topics in a tweet.

Summary

As we come to the end of our week looking at business writing, we have begun to explore the world of social media. This is a relatively new area but has become immensely popular recently and is certain not only to continue but also to develop in even further ways.

As an effective manager, you will want to engage with your potential and existing customers using online social media. It can be very useful to think which online media networks will be most profitable both in the short term (spreading the message now) and in the medium and long terms (maintaining good business relationships).

SUNDAY

MONDAY

TUESDAY

WEDNESDAY

THURSDAY

FRIDAY

SATURDAY

Fact-check [answers at the back]

1. Social media are:
a) a short-lived part of my marketing strategy ❑
b) an important part of my marketing strategy ❑
c) the only part of my marketing strategy ❑
d) not part of my thinking at all ❑

2. I use social media in my work:
a) as the only means of business communication ❑
b) not at all ❑
c) to interact with potential and existing clients ❑
d) for a laugh ❑

3. As regards social media:
a) I might get round to it one day ❑
b) I have a well-thought-out plan as to how to make most effective use of them ❑
c) I just muddle through ❑
d) I only use Facebook for personal stuff ❑

4. When writing text for social media:
a) I just write and hope for the best ❑
b) I'm a perfectionist so never make any mistakes, but I only write 100 words a day ❑
c) I plan my writing well and check it ❑
d) I forget any grammar I knew ❑

5. When writing for social media I adapt my style and tone to:
a) the audience I am writing to ❑
b) suit my personality ❑
c) my mood ❑
d) the weather ❑

6. I've joined:
a) more discussion groups than you ❑
b) so many discussion groups that I spend all day on them and neglect my real work ❑
c) no discussion groups at all ❑
d) a few well-chosen discussion groups ❑

7. Once I've written my content:
a) I keep it up to date ❑
b) I'm a perfectionist so I keep rewriting it ❑
c) I forget about it. I think I wrote something last year – I can't remember ❑
d) I press 'send' and hope for the best ❑

8. I network:
a) with other contacts constantly so that I never have time for my real work ❑
b) rarely ❑
c) never ❑
d) with other contacts regularly ❑

9. My profile:
a) is like my colleagues' ❑
b) doesn't exist yet ❑
c) reflects my current skills and experience ❑
d) is out of date ❑

10. As regards blogging:
a) I think I started one last year; I can't remember ❑
b) I write a blog every week to express my thoughts ❑
c) I haven't any time for that rubbish ❑
d) I spend all my time blogging; I never meet anyone in real life ❑

SUNDAY

MONDAY

TUESDAY

WEDNESDAY

THURSDAY

FRIDAY

SATURDAY

Follow-up

1 What are your overall business aims? In what ways can online social media help you fulfil those aims?
2 Who do you want to reach? What are your key messages? What do you want your readers to do after they have read your information?
3 Which social media will fit best with the responses you have given to questions 1 and 2?
4 If you currently use social media in your business, how effective are they? What objective evidence do you have for this?

SUNDAY

MONDAY

TUESDAY

WEDNESDAY

THURSDAY

FRIDAY

SATURDAY

Surviving in tough times

During an economic recession, effective business writing becomes even more important. Organizations that recognize that good business communication is essential are more likely to survive and prosper than those that don't. Managers in organizations that value communication know that effective emails, reports, etc. make the organization run more smoothly. More than that, good business writing also enables business with external clients to develop well.

As a manager, your role in ensuring effective business writing is critical. As well as being a role model for the team below you, you are also the channel for passing on information from higher in the organization. Here are ten crucial tips to help you make sure that you are an effective writer in tough times.

1 Know your aims

Be crystal clear about what the purpose of your email, report, presentation or website is. If necessary, discuss this with colleagues and refine it so that you can summarize your purpose in 12 words. Remember: time is money, so make the best of your time and that of your colleagues too.

2 Plan what you want to write

Do you remember being told at school to plan your essay or assignment, and you thought it a waste of time? So you launched straight in, only to find after a short time that you didn't know where you were in your argument. So after establishing your aims, plan what you want to write: think creatively and then organize your points logically.

3 Know your audience

Focus on them, not on yourself. What do you know about the colleagues you are trying to communicate to? How much do they know about what you are trying to communicate to them? Put yourself in their shoes as you begin to prepare an email, report, presentation, advertisement, press release, website or blog.

4 Listen well

Listening means not only that you affirm and value other people but also that you can discern how receptive colleagues are to new ideas and what you are trying to communicate. Furthermore, by listening, you can detect new industry trends and potential gaps in the market.

5 Know your message

Think about exactly what it is that you are trying to communicate. Then, having worked out your key message, break it down into small steps. Anticipate any objections the colleagues you are writing to might raise; prepare for them in advance.

6 Know what response you want

Know what response you want from the person you are communicating to, whether it is in an email, report, presentation, advertisement, press release, website or blog.

What are the next steps you want them to take? Make it as easy as possible for them to know what the next steps are and how you want them to respond.

7 Communicate using a variety of methods

Choose the best medium for your message, e.g. email, phone, face to face, or online social media. Email is a good all-round medium but is not the only way. Phoning is good to check someone has understood your message and also to build relationships. If you have to break difficult news, face to face is best. Don't rely only on email; use a range of ways of communicating.

8 Spend time fashioning your words carefully and skilfully

Make sure your content says exactly what you want it to say and that all your steps are logically ordered. Do not give in to the temptation to cut corners and leave a text unedited. Check and revise your email or report before you press 'send'.

9 Get the tone of your communications right

Whether it's an email, report, press release, advertisement or page on your website, check that the tone and level of formality and informality is appropriate to your message.

10 Write persuasively

Remember that business is built on confidence and perception, so you need to be able to inspire confidence in your readers. Argue convincingly. Present facts in a positive, enthusiastic and inspiring way. Emphasize benefits to your customers rather than features.

Answers

Sunday: 1d; 2b; 3d; 4a; 5c; 6b; 7b; 8c; 9a; 10b.

Monday: 1d; 2c; 3d; 4c; 5a; 6d; 7b; 8b; 9c; 10b.

Tuesday: 1d; 2b; 3c; 4d; 5c; 6b; 7b; 8a; 9c; 10a.

Wednesday: 1a; 2d; 3b; 4b; 5a; 6c; 7d; 8d; 9a; 10c.

Thursday: 1b; 2c; 3d; 4a; 5d; 6b; 7c; 8a; 9c; 10b.

Friday: 1c; 2a; 3d; 4b; 5b; 6a; 7c; 8a; 9c; 10d.

Saturday: 1b; 2c; 3b; 4c; 5a; 6d; 7a; 8d; 9c; 10b.